The Church of England Eucharist

1958-2012

Colin Buchanan

Retired Bishop of the Church of England
Member of the Liturgical Commission 1964-86

and

Trevor Lloyd

Retired Archdeacon of the Church of England
Member of the Liturgical Commission 1980-2002

ACKNOWLEDGMENTS

We are both deeply indebted to generations of members of the Liturgical Commission, the Revision Committees, and the Synod staff for the learning and experience gained from each of them, many of them now dead. We are also grateful to the members of the Alcuin/GROW Editorial Board who have reviewed our work helpfully during its compilation. And we have been greatly helped in recent correspondence with Shayne Ardron, Christopher Cocksworth, James Jones and David Stancliffe, each of whom has contributed from personal involvement in the production of the Common Worship liturgical provision.

Colin Buchanan

Trevor Lloyd

Passiontide 2019

The cover picture is a photo by Colin Buchanan of a Bradford church with the table prepaed for the eucharist.

ISSN: 0951-2667
ISBN: 978-0-334-05583-9

Contents

Coding of Rites

The coding below is followed throughout this Study. The bold codes against the left margin are definitive forms, representing the conclusion of a particular revision process, and in all cases except 1928 and 1995-96 actually reaching authorization for use. The use of bold type, as, e.g. 1549, specifically means the communion rite of that year, and in ordinary type ('1549') it means either the year, or sometimes the whole Book of that year. The indented codes in lighter type represent texts which came into the public arena as part of the process leading to the next bold code below them, and are therefore part of the story, illuminating the various stages in the processes. Where rites contained more than one eucharistic prayer, then the coding (whether by number or letter) is shown in brackets after the code for the text.

1548	RtA/79(1-4)(Series 3 revised accepted in 1979)
1549	**RtA/80 (1-4)** (Rite A in ASB 1980)
1552	BCP-Order 'The Order following the Pattern of the Book of Common Prayer' (In Rite A in ASB)
1559	RtB/78 (1-2) (Series 1-2 revised proposal)
1604	**RtB/80 (1-2)** (Rite B in ASB 1980)
1637	RtC/89 (1-4) (Rite C proposed in *Patterns for Worship* 1989)
1662	
1927 (the BCP as proposed in 1927)	EPs/92 (1-4) (Rite C prayers retouched for House of Bishops 1992)
1928	EPs/94(1-5) (Rite C prayers further retouched for the Bishops 1994)
IntrmRt (1939)	
S1/65 (Series 1 proposals in 1965)	EPs(HB)/94(1-2) (EPs/94 reduced to two by Bishops)
S1/66 (Series 1 as authorized in 1966)	**95-96(1-6)** (Six alternative eucharistic prayers proposed to Synod and defeated in 1996)
S2/65 (Series 2 'draft order' in 1965)	
S2/66 (Series 2 proposal in 1966)	CW/98 (A-F)(Six different eucharistic prayers proposed for Common Worship 1998)
S2/67 (Series 2 as authorized in 1967)	
S3/71 (Series 3 proposal in 1971)	CW/99 (A-F) (CW/98 as amended in Revision Committee 1999)
S3/73 (Series 3 as authorized in 1973)	
S1-2/75(1-2) (Series 1 & 2 proposal in 1975)	**CW/00 (A-H)** (Order One as authorized within Common Worship 2000)
S1-2/76(1-2)(Series 1 & 2 as authorized in 1976)	**CW/00 (OrdOneTrad)**
RtA/78(1-3)(Series 3 revised proposal in 1978)	**CW/00 (OrdTwo)**; **CW/00(OrdTwoContmp)**

Note: the three Houses of the pre-1970 Church Assembly and of the post-1970 General Synod are distinguished by the use of capitals. Thus 'Bishops' means 'House of Bishops', whereas 'bishops' is simply the plural of 'bishop'. Voting figures are given in the order: Bishops: Clergy: Laity

Abbreviations

ARCIC	Anglican-Roman Catholic International Commission
ASB	Alternative Service Book
BCP	Book of Common Prayer
BCP-Order	The Order following the Pattern of the Book of Common Prayer
CHP	Church House Publishing
CIO	Church Information Office
CSI	Church of South India
CW	Common Worship
ELLC	English Language Liturgical Consultation (ecumenical)
IALC	International Anglican Liturgical Consultation
ICEL	International Commission on English in the Liturgy (Roman Catholic)
ICET	International Consultation on English Texts (ecumenical)
LHWE	*Lent – Holy Week - Easter*
NOL	*News of Liturgy*
PBS	Prayer Book Society
SPCK	Society for the Promotion of Christian Knowledge
TEC	The Episcopal Church (USA)
UPA	Urban Priority Areas

Introduction

Within the Church of England liturgical texts have importance, not only for public worship, but also as the public face of the Church's doctrine, identifying its character. This has been peculiarly so with the communion service, because of its prominence in worship, but also as for nearly two centuries a focus of doctrinal controversy. We were both ordained when **1662**, still very largely Cranmer's rite of **1552**, was the only authorized eucharistic use; and so we tell at first hand the history of our changing eucharistic texts since those last days of Uniformity. We have both seen that sequence unfold, and have ourselves lived within that unfolding process, seeing it from the inside, and contributing vigorously ourselves to its character.[1] Colin Buchanan was on the Liturgical Commission from 1964 to 1986 during the formative years of the ASB; Trevor Lloyd was on the Commission from 1981 to 2002 during the creation of the major Common Worship volumes. We have spent long days (and not a few late nights) in General Synod and its Revision Committees; and have stumped the country and written extensively to assist the intelligent introduction of the new rites being authorized. As participants, we are no dispassionate observers, and our value-judgments, as those of any historian, may occasionally show. Our fellow-members of the Joint Editorial Board may well embrace different value-judgments, but they have commissioned us for the task, and have also been willing to charter a double-size Study so as to carry the story in some detail within a single volume.

The background to the post-war liturgical changes explored here is the defeat in Parliament of the 1928 'Proposed' BCP. The shortcomings of that Book, the years of conflict about it, and the reasons for its defeat

---

[1]   We have also taken a major part through these 60 years in recording and publicizing liturgical reform in the Church of England – see the select bibliography on pp.127-128.

are all recorded elsewhere.[2] The defeat left the Bishops to devise an emergency policy, to steer the Church between the unwelcome anarchy for which the bolder anglo-catholics were calling and the impossible conformity to 1662 for which more protestant voices in both Church and nation were raised. The bishops sounded out their dioceses and initiated an improvised policy with three strands:

First, they would seek for substantial printing of the 1928 Book, called the 'Deposited' Book, with a disclaimer included that stated that it had no legal authority for use;

Secondly, they would issue a statement saying that they would not 'regard as inconsistent with loyalty to the principles of the Church of England the use of such additions or deviations as fall within the limits' of the 1928 Book.

Thirdly, they would never again send liturgy to Parliament, but would seek legal ways by which services could be authorized by the Church's own procedures.

As the bishops were claiming some kind of *ius liturgicum*, through the 1930s the clergy came broadly to believe that the bishop as Ordinary could approve the use of services other than the 1662 ones, and regularly used both 1662 and 1928 services.[3] There was little love for the 1928 Prayer of Consecration, but the Prayer for the Church (no longer just 'Militant here on Earth') was widely adopted. The third strand of the policy led to the Church and State Report of 1935. This recommended revisiting the 1604 Canons; and that led to a Canon Law Commission

---

[2] See, e.g. Donald Gray, *The 1927-28 Prayer Book Crisis*, two volumes, nos 60 (2005) and 61 (2006) in these Alcuin/GROW Joint Liturgical Studies (Hymns Ancient & Modern, Norwich); also a fuller study in John Maiden, *National Religion and the Prayer Book Controversy, 1927-1928* (Studies in Modern British Religious History, Boydell, 2009).

[3] This was grounded in the exceptive clause provided in the 1865 Declaration of Assent inserted as Canon 36 into the 1604 Code: 'I will use the form in the said Book provided except so far as shall be ordered by lawful authority'. There was a readiness to believe the bishop was that 'lawful authority' but it was a very doubtful interpretation of the law.

in 1939.[4] This Commission, interrupted by the War, reported in 1947, and the Church Assembly plodded slowly through 17 years to bring the legislation amending the 1662 Act of Uniformity before Parliament. Parliament accepted the Church of England (Alternative and Other Services) Measure in 1965; the Canons to implement it were approved; the monarch ordered their promulgation; the archbishops named the date; and provision for 'alternative services' finally began on 1 May 1966.

1662 was still entrenched in the public perception in the 1960s. Gregory Dix had insisted in *The Shape of the Liturgy* that the rite was Zwinglian, and could not be retrieved or restored to 'Catholic' orthodoxy. Yet the tercentenary of the 1662 Book was celebrated in 1962 with public lectures, published as *The English Prayer Book 1549-1662* (Alcuin/SPCK, 1963); the major contributor on 1662 itself was Geoffrey Cuming, who had edited *The Durham Book* (Oxford, 1960), and later wrote extensively on the BCP. Bernard Wigan put together all Anglican eucharistic texts since 1549 in *The Liturgy in English* (Oxford, 1962). Arthur Couratin turned two journal articles into *The Service of Holy Communion 1549-1662* (SPCK, 1963); whereas Martin Parsons wrote a practical guide in *Holy Communion* (Hodder & Stoughton, 1963) for the many who still valued and used it.

However it was not solely, nor even primarily, academic enquiry which inspired the revision process we trace here. The growth in the parish communion in the post-war years meant rising numbers worshipped weekly at a 'main service' communion; and it was **1662** which each Sunday provided their sole liturgical diet. Within the run of 'Parish Communion' parishes reforming spirits sometimes addressed offertory processions and Westward position for the president, but textual change was the centre of attention. The critics said that **1662**, whatever the merits of its theology and the incomparability of its prose, had an inadequate

---

[4] For the slow development of any policies which related to the eucharist, see R.C.D.Jasper, *The Development of the Anglican Liturgy 1662-1980* (SPCK, 1989) pp.147-153.

lectionary, a rigid form of intercessions, a narrow doctrinal concentration upon the atonement, an inexplicable shape to its sacramental section, a monopolistic role for the president (and correspondingly minimal participation by the congregation), and even (though this dawned a little later) an unnecessarily Tudor character to its language. They wished the church to participate in its liturgy, not simply attend it. So ending legal barriers to alternative rites was certain to stimulate a strong groundswell for new liturgical texts. The archbishops in the 1960s took the point; the task was commissioned; thereafter it could hardly be reversed; and this Study records how, in respect of the eucharist, it went.

We note in passing that the whole revision process within the Church of England from the 1950s to 2012 ran with little reference to ecumenical considerations or to Anglican uses elsewhere. The major exceptions to this were: firstly, an awareness of changes in Rome (with strong advocacy of particular Roman uses by a few determined Synod members); secondly, a welcome in principle to the international ecumenical texts;[5] and, thirdly, a concern in the post-1986 Commission to engage with both IALC and ICEL publications and Anglican rites in Canada and New Zealand. Other Anglican provinces have drawn on Church of England texts, but the reverse has not often been the case. Revision here tends to proceed in a self-sufficient way, in dialogue with its own past, but rarely looking beyond its own borders: Hippolytus (co-called) makes a contribution, and the Liturgy of St Basil receives a passing nod, but even they are but starting-points for self-contained English Anglicanism to devise its own formulations.

With the advice of the Joint Editorial Board we have structured the account so that Part 1 provides a necessary historical framework, but the major treatment of the theological and liturgical issues which relate to eucharistic texts comes in Part 2.

---

[5] See Appendix on p.124.

Part I
Historical Outline

1. Early stages

Before World War II, live concern for revision of the eucharist came largely from anglo-catholics. Bolder spirits wanted to imitate Rome, others looked towards overseas Anglican rites, and the less radical favoured the 'interim rite' (IntrmRt); that is, **1662** reshuffled to provide a 'long prayer' of consecration, with the first alternative prayer after communion, the 'prayer of oblation', brought into its latter part.[6] There were moves in the Convocations in 1941-42 to get such a rite approved for use.[7] Dix, however, sounded a slow death-knell for such a proposal: 'if you share Cranmer's theology, you would do much better to follow his form of the rite; if you do not follow it, you will not achieve what you want by shuffling his wording around'.[8]

So how was a revised rite to be provided? During the 1950s the slow reform of the Canons meant light at the end of the tunnel – church-authorization of alternative services was coming into view, later into law. No revision was occurring yet in Rome – Vatican II still lay in an

---

[6] This pattern is usually traced back to Frere's suggestion in *Some Principles of Liturgical Reform* (John Murray, London, 1911) pp.190-194. He was attempting to keep Cranmer's wording within a structure more like 1549 . The title 'Interim Rite', was popularized when given to an alternative text within a revised edition of *The Anglican Missal* in 1939. 'Interim' clearly indicated hopes of more thoroughgoing revision .

[7] We say 'approved', as actual authority for liturgy would still have been needed from Parliament. The Church Assembly was not going to send any Measure there. 1927-28 remained a very vivid memory!

[8] G.N.Dix, *The Shape of the Liturgy* (Dacre, London, 1945) p.692, fn 1.

unforeseen future.[9] However, there was interest in the new creative rite produced in 1950 in the newly united Church of South India. This was for use at their synod and similar occasions to transcend the inherited traditions of those who had been Anglican, Methodist or Reformed before 1947. They followed Dix's guidance on 'shape', and also advocated active sharing of the Peace and westward-facing for the president.[10]

In 1954 the Convocations asked the archbishops to form a Liturgical Commission, to prepare draft proposals ready for authorization when the canonical day dawned. The archbishops appointed Colin Dunlop, Dean of Lincoln, to chair the Commission which first met in December 1955.[11] They were asked to produce a report for the 1958 Lambeth Conference, and they themselves sought the goodwill of the archbishops to draft wholly new proposals for baptism and confirmation. These two initial tasks precluded their quickly addressing the eucharist.

Their report, *Liturgical Revision in the Church of England* (CIO, 1957), surveyed events before and after 1928, then offered some 'Guiding Principles' for future revision – the first being 'Prayer Book Revision should be conservative'. The Conference also received a longer report from the Church of India, Pakistan, Burma and Ceylon, *Principles of Prayer Book Revision* (CIO, 1957). The sub-section addressing Prayer Book Revision drew upon both reports, and reported with advice much quoted in later years:

We desire to draw attention to a conception of consecration which is scriptural and primitive and goes behind subsequent controversies with respect to the moment and formula of consecration. This is

---

[9] Pius XII had relaxed the laws on fasting communion and revised the Holy Week rites, including changing the timing of the Easter Eve ceremonies. But these reforms carried no inherent promise of revision of major texts of 1500 years standing..

[10] See T.Garrett, *Worship in the Church of South India* (Lutterworth, 1958) pp.28-29, and Leslie Brown, *Relevant Liturgy* (Oxford, 1964) pp.60-61.

[11] He had been Bishop of Jarrow 1944-50, before becoming Dean of Lincoln.

associated with the Jewish origin of eucharistia and may be called consecration through thanksgiving.[12]

They also asserted a principle of liturgical revision, not drawn from the two reports, but reflecting current Anglican thinking:

It was Cranmer's aim to lift worship in England out of the liturgical decadence of the late medieval Church in western Christendom, and to recover as much as possible of the character of the worship of what he called the 'Primitive Church'. In this he achieved notable success, but there was not available in his day the historical material necessary for the full accomplishment of his aim. Since that time, and indeed since 1662, valuable evidence has been brought to light, by the use of which what he began may be developed.[13]

This latter quotation somewhat misrepresents Cranmer and wholly overstates contemporary certainty about patristic uses, but it mirrors the atmosphere and groundrules within which the Commission was operating: adopting early liturgical forms would not only restore original Christian usage, but would also 'get behind' polarizing Reformation conflicts, and would thus transcend disagreed positions among Anglicans.

The Commission soon ran into trouble. Their baptism and confirmation drafts, published in 1958, roused conflict in the Convocation of York in 1960. The Commission was reconstituted; Donald Coggan, Bishop of Bradford, became chairman; some personnel were changed; appointments now became time-limited. Leaving baptism aside, in 1960 Archbishop Fisher still wished the Commission to observe as a priority

---

[12] *The Lambeth Conference 1958* (SPCK, 1958) p.2.85 (it was not wholly new, being articulated, e.g., in South Africa concerning the experimental rite authorized in 1924).

[13] *Ibid.*, p.2.81

for the eucharist a 'schedule of variants' on **1662**, thus authorizing IntrmRt or something like it. The Commission replied that this was a short-term policy, and repeated their expectation of being asked for 'fully revised services'. However, the next two years were spent on relatively undemanding tasks; but in 1962, after changes brought in lay members including women, they addressed revision of the eucharist. The drafting was done by Arthur Couratin, resigning then as principal of St Stephen's House to become canon-residentiary in Durham. He echoed Dix's verdict on Cranmer, attached great authority to so-called Hippolytus, and was well informed about anglo-catholic concerns - he had himself instilled them in many ordinands. That Summer he brought questions about the structure and contents of the eucharist to the Commission for discussion. Without agreeing a set of principles, the Commission set in hand two booklets for public discussion, and returned to polishing other proposed services.

The two booklets were published around July 1964 by the CIO, *Why Prayer Book Revision at all?* by Basil Naylor; and *Re-shaping the Liturgy*, by Henry de Candole and Arthur Couratin. The former hardly bore upon eucharistic revision; the latter concentrated on it. *Re-shaping* identified the various parts of the liturgy, and then asked questions about their content and significance, thus echoing Couratin's questions to the Commission. However, the section on 'The Meal' named four elements in the sacramental order: the Offertory, the Thanksgiving or Consecration, the Breaking of the Bread, and Communion. This identification, echoing Dix's 'shape', was unlike **1662** or even IntrmRt, but was assumed as a 'given' for the basic structure of the eucharist. The booklet's questions came within those categories, which themselves remained unquestioned.[14]

Meanwhile Couratin was drafting an actual text, and in September 1964 (when Colin Buchanan joined the Commission and Ronald Jasper succeeded Donald Coggan as chairman) he presented a full

---

[14] See the fuller account of the 'fourfold action' in Part 2, chapter 7 below.

draft of a radically new eucharistic text. The archbishops were pressing the Commission to have draft proposals ready for authorization when the Prayer Book (Alternative and Other Services) Measure, already adopted by the Church Assembly, should become law, as Parliamentary assent was sure in 1965.[15] The archbishops were naming 1 May 1966 as the starting date; and consequently wanted proposals by late 1965. With Jasper they planned two 'series' of services – 'First Series' being essentially the 1928 rites which, to become lawful, would need full legal authorization; otherwise the new canonical dispensation would be flouted from the outset – for the Measure abolished any *fiat* of a diocesan bishop. However, few, if any, actually wanted **1928**, and so attention turned to some form of IntrmRt (though including, e.g., the **1928** Prayer for the Church). The archbishops asked the Commission to edit the texts for First Series – and the Commission declined! Their apathy towards Fisher's 'schedule of variants' was unwavering; they professed no love for 1928-type services; they would not be responsible for them; indeed they feared lest debates on those rites would pre-empt proper consideration of their own 'Second Series' proposals. So First Series proposals emerged in December 1965, as 'the result of long consideration by the Bishops, and of consultation with some members of the Liturgical Commission and of the Joint Liturgical Steering Committee of the Convocations'.[16] The proposed eucharistic rite was a form of IntrmRt. But the Commission, uncluttered by First Series, spent each meeting combing over Couratin's draft for Second Series, with Couratin himself re-drafting in the light of discussion.

The Commission was pressed in 1965 not only by the legislative timetable, but also by emerging prospective changes in Rome. At the

---

[15] An election was due and the Convocations had been dissolved along with the House of Commons, and an election of proctors was due straight after the Parliamentary election. The House of Laity sat for secure quinquennial periods; with no election due until Autumn 1965.

[16] *Alternative Services: First Series* (SPCK, 1965) Preface. The editing was almost certainly far hastier than the careful wording conveys.

June meeting the draft text briefly exhibited a complete blank in the intercessions section. Rome was drafting a sequence of extemporary biddings, set petition, and versicle and response, and this challenged the Commission's work. With much unresolved, the Commission reported in September that they had not yet agreed their eucharistic rite, and the archbishops instructed them to publish a text, however provisional, even if not signed off as agreed. Thus the 'Second Series' services in December 1965 included agreed proposals for Morning and Evening Prayer and Burial (and Churching of Women), but then simply 'A Draft Order for Holy Communion: An Interim Report...'[17] That 'interim' reflected pressures of time and of changes in Rome, but also Colin Buchanan's doctrinal disagreement with the draft; this was, however, not overt in an unsigned draft.

The Convocations and Laity arranged a semi-informal 'Liturgical Conference' between themselves and the Commission on 17-18 February 1966 to consider First and Second Series. At this Couratin commended the draft eucharistic rite, as enabling all strands of Anglicans to worship with it, perhaps with some minimal discomfort. Little criticism was voiced, and the main vigorous response was 'Don't spend more time polishing it – finish it for us as quickly as possible.'[18] The new canonical provision was to begin on 1 May, so the Commission meeting at the end of March would inevitably be pressed by the archbishops to provide a finished eucharistic text then.

On the Commission Colin Buchanan had opposed the petition for the departed within the intercessions and the (Hippolytan-based) oblation of the bread and cup within the anamnesis, both as lacking scriptural warrant, and as incompatible with Anglican doctrine or **1662**. After the Liturgical Conference, at a conference of younger evangelical clergy, he

---

[17] *Alternative Services: Second Series* (SPCK, 1965) p.145
[18] See the verbatim report, *The Liturgical Conference 1966: Report of Proceedings* (CIO, 1966) pp.70-87

asked them as neutrally as possible how they viewed the draft rite. The response to his questionnaire was overwhelmingly opposed to both the petition for the departed and the oblation of the elements. He thus knew, when the Commission met, that he was not making an eccentric stand through some theory of his own, but his theological sticking-points genuinely represented a swathe of Anglican conviction, unnoticed by the Commission. While regretting other features of the draft (as, e.g., the loss of 'by his one oblation of himself once offered, etc.'), he confined his opposition to these two major features; and, when his alternative proposals were rejected, he then dissented. With debates in early May in prospect, he swiftly wrote up his dissent, and through generous donations this was published and posted to the 700 members of the Convocations and Laity before 1 May.[19] The Convocation debate itself had enough voices calling for an agreed solution to justify an adjournment; and a working party was to address the text of the anamnesis. In October the Convocations viewed this working party's proposal as clumsy and instead provided alternative main verbs in the anamnesis – either 'we offer unto thee this bread and this cup' or 'we give thanks to thee over this bread and this cup'. Thus it was sent to the Laity.

The Laity, however, would not comply: alternatives, if any, should all be usable by all, and not appear on a 'one for you and one for me' basis.[20] The Convocations were slower to adopt this principle, but had to learn. The Laity in February 1967 asked for the Liturgical Conference, scheduled for April to discuss initiation proposals, to include time to revisit this

---

[19] Colin Buchanan, *The New Communion Service – Reasons for Dissent* (Church Book Room Press, 1966), also published in *Churchman* (Summer 1966) and then in Colin Buchanan's Alcuin Collection, *An Evangelical Among the Anglican Liturgists* (SPCK, 2009).

[20] This was in clear contrast with the Laity's readiness for split votes and bare two-thirds majorities when handling the 1928-cum-Series 1 texts in 1966. There the majority had simply reckoned that texts already widely in use should be legitimized to begin the new era; but the majority had not enjoyed hurting that minority who opposed in conscience the doctrinal character of the proposed texts; and so they wanted to authorize new texts by near-consensus. This principle governed most liturgical revision from that time onwards.

split over the eucharist. At the Conference on 25 April the basic text of **1549** ('with this bread and this cup we make the memorial') gathered sufficient support from churchpeople of all persuasions to indicate an agreed way forward.[21] A similar amelioration in respect of the petition for the departed was also advocated. The Convocations amended the text the next day and returned it to the Laity. The Laity accepted it by 185-8 on 7 July 1967, and authorized it for a four-year period. The blue booklet was published on 7 September.

On the Commission Ronald Jasper could be glad that the stopgap text at least enabled the new era of alternative services to begin. However, in June 1967 Edward Ratcliff died; and in July Arthur Couratin, bereft of both Ratcliff, his much trusted older colleague, and also the oblation of the bread and cup, the text he valued so highly, resigned from the Commission. After Ratcliff and Couratin there came a change of atmosphere; and a change of language was also imminent.[22]

2. Modern Language

In 1968 came the language change. It affected liturgy throughout the English-speaking world, and across the different Christian denominations. Interestingly the Commission had discussed it back in 1960, but no drafting had then been attempted.[23] The key to it was eliminating the traditional 'thou', 'thee', 'thy' and 'thine' in relation to God. Deeply though Tudor language might be entrenched in people's devotions, there was no biblical justification for a distinctive language for addressing God; and at root the issue was largely one of aesthetic taste

---

[21] Colin Buchanan recalls Maurice Wood (then principal of Oak Hill and one of the few evangelical members of the Convocations) finding him in the wings and asking 'Can we accept this?' to which he replied 'You had better, lest worse befall.'

[22] A concurrent small change of conventions renamed 'First Series' as 'Series 1' and 'Second Series' as 'Series 2'.

[23] J.B.Phillips, famed for pioneering modern language translations of the New Testament, was approached. However, his drafted sample prayer mirrored Tudor, not contemporary, liturgical language.

rather than theological principle. 1662 and Series 1 rites were going to continue in use, so, where PCCs were agreed, these rites could cater for them. But the Commission, with clear directives from the archbishops, was to address modern language. The point was emphasized by the nomination of a creative young English don from Cambridge, David Frost, to join the Commission at the next three-year starting-point, Autumn 1968.

The Commission without waiting for his appointment published in Spring 1968 *Modern Liturgical Texts* (SPCK). This bore upon the eucharist in two ways. First it included the Commission's initial drafts of modern-language liturgical texts with ecumenical implications, notably Gloria in Excelsis, Nicene Creed, Sanctus and the Lord's Prayer, each new translation with a commentary.[24] These texts became the Commission's first contribution to the work of the newly forming International Consultation on English Texts (ICET). Secondly the booklet included Series 2 communion 'translated' by Geoffrey Cuming (though he was not named) into modern language.

With a changed team and a changed language Ronald Jasper began from scratch to create a eucharistic prayer to be welcomed and used in all parts of the Church. He did the drafting himself and, viewing the anamnesis as needing the most sensitive drafting, he began a correspondence with Kenneth Ross of All Saints, Margaret Street, and with Colin Buchanan. An agreed text resulted and was hailed as a 'great improvement' by Michael Ramsey.[25] A key feature was superseding the makeshift 'we make the memorial' with 'we celebrate'. A poignant sequel was that Kenneth Ross died just two days after sending his assent to Ronald Jasper in May 1970.

Early in 1970 ICET produced its first definitive texts for Gloria in

---

[24] The Lord's Prayer and its commentary were crafted by the remarkable Austin Farrer, shortly before he died.
[25] See Ronald Jasper, *The Development of the Anglican Liturgy 1662-1980* (SPCK, 1989), p.310

Excelsis, Sanctus, the Lord's Prayer etc. in *Prayers We Have in Common*. No publicity accompanied the publication, and the Commission proposed that the modern texts should only be considered within their projected Series 3 communion. 18 months elapsed and the ICET texts remained unknown. However the full eucharistic text was taking shape from different sources: Geoffrey Cuming's draft in *Modern Liturgical Texts*; these ICET texts; sensitive drafting such as had provided the eucharistic prayer; and an enrichment in three new compositions by David Frost: alternative forms of humble access, of the confession, and of a post-communion prayer. The presentation was also updated – general notes at the beginning made some rubrics unnecessary and 'lining' in bold type was introduced for congregational texts. The Commission published its *Commentary* alongside it; and thus the first modern language proposal, S3/71, appeared in September 1971. General Synod had two revision stages, and the text was heavily criticized (not least for the 'Frost' prayers) at the first debate.[26] However, milder counsels prevailed thereafter; there was some sensible amending; and final approval with little dissent came on 7 November 1972.[27] **S3/73** in a green booklet would run for four years from 1 February 1973. Ronald Jasper followed its publication with a weighty set of essays, *The Eucharist Today: Studies on Series 3* (SPCK, 1974).[28]

However, although **S3/73** gained currency, a broad swathe of

---

[26] In what was experienced as corporate emotion, the Synod's mood most notably excised the first two 'Frost' prayers (time expired before they reached the post-communion one). The Commission dubbed it 'the night of the long knives'.

[27] Among the changes, the work of the Spirit was inserted into the first epiclesis (the mover citing the Anglican-Roman Catholic Agreement of 1971), and in the acclamations 'Christ will come again', as revived in CSI from the Liturgy of St James, was restored . The option of supplementary consecration in silence was removed (see chapter ll in Part 2 below)..

[28] Commission members wrote most chapters, but Paul Bradshaw's investigation of 'celebration' strongly supported the Commission's adoption of 'celebrate' as key verb in the anamnesis; and R.J.Halliburton, writing on 'The Canon of Series 3', linked the absence of manual acts with the Commission's concern to avoid 'the notion...that it is the recitation of the words of institution that effect the consecration of the elements' (*The Eucharist Today*, p.109).

Anglicans still treasured **S2/67**, not least for linguistic purposes. So did it need to lapse when its licence expired in 1971? Initially Synod gave it just one year, but in 1972 extended it to November 1976. Jasper planned to bring **S1/66** and **S2/67** (both in traditional language) within one structure which would provide, e.g., the Peace and then the fourfold eucharistic shape to follow it, with the eucharistic prayers from the two rites as alternatives within it. General Synod welcomed this policy and there duly emerged 'Series 1 and 2 Revised'.[29] It went through its stages in Synod in 1975 and 1976, and was authorized from 1 November 1976 to 31 December 1979 (**S1-2/76**).[30]

This end-date of December 1979 carried another message about developments. The Church of England (Worship and Doctrine) Measure 1974 came into force on 1 September 1975, and the Synod could now authorize services without time-limit. So Synod's working party addressing future policy recommended authorizing a hardback book of modern alternative services to give long-term stability. The proposed end of 1979 indicated the lead-time the authorities needed to prepare such a book.

Synod duly adopted in 1976 the plan for an 'Alternative Service Book'. The policy was that all other Series 3 (ie modern language) services after **S3/73**, would be marginally 'adapted' for consistency without further revision. But **S3/73**, with a sufficient time for trial use, would incur full-scale revision, stemming from the Commission, but then undergoing the whole synodical process. The Commission put out questionnaires in

---

[29] One change made to the **S2/67** prayer in **S1-2/76** was to add 'the power of thy Holy Spirit' in the first epiclesis, mirroring the change effected in **S3/73**, mentioned in note 27 above. See further on the epiclesis in chapter 11 in part 2 below.

[30] As a tidying up exercise it never acquired enthusiastic support, and some controversial features of **S1/66** still aroused opposition. At the last stage the Bishops made further changes which increased disquiet in Synod, and its two-thirds majority in the Clergy on final approval came by 105-52; Colin Buchanan, on the Steering Committee, abstained, and Geoffrey Cuming, being lame, decided against ascending the great flight of steps at York to go through the 'no' door. Either of these voting against it would have defeated it. As it was, it survived.

1976-77, and learned of widespread satisfaction with **S3/73** among those who used it (others did not receive the questionnaire). The sole widely disliked feature was the modern Lord's Prayer.[31]

By the end of 1977 the Commission had completed its redrafting. It ran into trouble with the Bishops, who wished that main verb of the anamnesis to revert to 'we make the memorial', the very text the Commission had with relief superseded in **S3/73**. The Commission, when faced with this reversal, declined to sign the report. Time pressed, and the four bishops handling the relationships obtained by correspondence the House's agreement to the Commission's (slightly altered) text. 'We celebrate' stood; and the text was duly signed. It was scheduled for the Synod debate on General Approval in July 1978. Colin Buchanan was appointed chair of the steering committee.

3. The Eucharist in the ASB

Colin Buchanan introduced RtA/78 on 11 July 1978, commending it both for its intrinsic merits and as arising from over five years' experience of using **S3/73**. Synod welcomed it enthusiastically, and duly remitted it to a Revision Committee to prepare for the one Revision Stage in Synod. Around 1200 proposed amendments flooded the Committee, which sat that Autumn for 15 separate days. Rather than vote on these *seriatim*, the Steering Committee drafted before each meeting a 'mainstream' text, to mop up many amendments, and thus to reduce the actual voting that was needed.

Obviously, a major feature of the revision was the eucharistic prayer. The Commission had not only re-touched the eucharistic prayer in **S3/73** (and defied the Bishops), but had also considered both worshippers who wanted **S2/67** unrevised but in modern dress, and others who similarly wanted **S1/66** in modern dress, to preserve the style of Cranmer and IntrmRt . These were the First, Second and Third Eucharistic Prayers in

---

[31] See the Appendix on Common Texts below.

RtA/78. An unexpected feature of the revision came from Brian Brindley, an anglo-catholic member of the Committee, and Roger Beckwith, the evangelical warden of Latimer House, Oxford. They together proposed both a new draft based upon the Roman Catholic Eucharistic Prayer II, itself a latterday Roman recension of Hippolytus' eucharistic prayer, and also a modernized **1662**, requesting that in equity the revised text should include both. Neither was likely to use the text the other wanted – it was, in words Roger Beckwith used in public, 'horse-trading', exactly the 'one for you and one for me' procedure which the Commission (and the Synod) had eschewed.[32] The Revision Committee accepted the double proposal, but first re-touched the Brindley Hippolytan text. This became the Third Eucharistic Prayer in the revised text, with the modernized **S1/66** prayer consequently the Fourth. The modernized **1662** was printed after the rite as 'The Order following the pattern of the Book of Common Prayer'; it branched from the main text after the intercession, and linguistically shared the wording of the Fourth Eucharistic Prayer.[33]

Other changes came from absorbing the flood of amendments. The eucharistic prayers were highly sensitive texts, but the Committee also faced controversy over the Creed (notably the *Filioque*), the Lord's Prayer (where 'Do not bring us to the time of trial' was disliked after six years of use), and the Roman 'Offertory Prayers' (desired by some, resisted by others). The Committee restored the two 'Frost' prayers which had been lost in the 'night of the long knives' in November 1971. They recommended texts for the Peace, fraction, distribution, post-

---

[32] It was not even fair horse-trading, as a modernized **1662** was already provided by rubrics in RtA/78.

[33] One variant from it concealed a slight smile behind the poker-faced recommendations of the Committee. Some submissions had suggested that the Commission's rubrical use of 'president' rather than 'priest', was surreptitiously allowing Methodist ministers or even lay persons to officiate at the eucharist.. The Committee then referred in the opening 'Notes' to Canon B12, requiring the president to be an episcopally ordained priest. However, to meet those worried people, they retained the BCP title 'priest' in the rubrics in BCP-Order. The slight smile reflected the awareness that those who most wanted to see 'priest' in the rubric were those least likely ever to use that 1662-style provision.

communion, and supplementary consecration. They provided 'proper' scriptural sentences to begin both the service and the post-communion. And for virtually every such text, they picked their way through a floor ankle-deep in mutually exclusive proposed amendments. By a day-and-night process they produced a lucid and careful RtA/79, somewhat changed from RtA/78, but enriched and with a strong consensus on the Committee to commend it.

So the Revision Committee in January 1979 sent RtA/79 to Synod. The members engaged vigorously with it, and submitted around 200 amendments. The Steering Committee tabled another 100 or so, sometimes to consolidate points from differing proposals, sometimes as their fall-back for damage-limitation if some amendment they resisted nevertheless carried the Synod. The Revision Stage of over 19 hours engulfed several hours each Synod day in both February and July. The final text on 6 July 1979, not far from RtA/79, but further polished and made internally consistent, then gained provisional approval with but one vote against. The Bishops reversed one minor decision of Synod; and Final Approval came on 7 November 1979 by: 33-3; 207-10; 150-23. Thus **RtA/80** was authorized for use from 1 May 1980, and included within the ten-year licence of the whole ASB from 10 November 1980. Where 'common texts' came in other ASB rites, **RtA/80** provided the model. This was of particular interest in its impact on the Lord's Prayer.

The contents of the ASB included an issue about 'traditional' language texts. The working party shaping the ASB recommended that **S1-2/76** could go into it, and it was duly adapted, and authorized for use in July 1979.[34] Colin Buchanan then moved in Synod to exclude it from the Book, and lost by 162-127, and it became **RtB/80**.[35]

---

[34] An unusual feature of this adaptation was that contemporary language proper prefaces drafted for **RiteA/80** were 'traditionalized' to provide a comparable selection to fit into the **S2/67** eucharistic prayer.

[35] He reasoned that lovers of the contemporary would not want the rite, and lovers of the traditional were unlikely to buy more than 1,000 pages of modern texts to get the rite they wanted (and

The ASB was launched on 10 November 1980. A companion to it, *The Alternative Service Book 1980: A Commentary by the Liturgical Commission* (SPCK), had a chapter on the eucharist drafted jointly by Colin Buchanan and David Silk.[36]

4. Developing from the ASB

For nine years no changes to the existing texts burst into sight.[37] It had been questioned in 1980 whether a new Liturgical Commission was needed, but one was duly appointed.[38] Then Douglas Jones, the new chairman, with Colin Buchanan and David Silk went to discuss their agenda with the Bishops, and of the possible tasks listed only one, Holy Week services, was completed in the next five years. However, they also addressed a topic which for some decades lurked around the Church of England, the practice of so-called 'concelebration'. Two Commission members, Trevor Lloyd and Hugh Wybrew, described by the chairman as representing 'different wings of Anglican churchmanship', wrote *Concelebration in the Eucharist* (GS (Misc) 163, November 1982), arguing

---

already possessed). But forces other than commonsense were at work – largely seeking a cosmetic gesture to reassure lovers of the traditional of their future in the worship and life of the Church. This process adumbrated events in the 1990s. **RtB/80** added 36 arguably redundant pages to the ASB.

[36] The *Commentary* relates to the thematic treatment in part 2 below. But we note here the opening of the paragraph on 'Consecration':

'The Eucharistic Prayer is not called in the rite "The Prayer of Consecration", but it is still viewed as "consecrating". The difference from the older views is that there is now no solemnly identified formula or "moment of consecration". Rather, the whole giving of thanks sets the theological context within which we can confidently assert that this is the communion of the body and blood of the Lord.' (*Commentary*, pp.78-79)

[37] In the first quinquennium Synod handled the communion of the sick, recommended by the previous Commission, and hardly involving change touching the eucharist. It did open the issue of reservation, discussed in Part 2, chapter 16, below.

[38] The Commission now ran in quinquennia following the Synod elections. 1981 saw great change in personnel; Ronald Jasper, Geoffrey Cuming and Charles Whitaker and others departed. The new chairman, Canon Douglas Jones, evinced recurrent concern for legitimizing the variant on **RtB/80** used in his Durham cathedral (and the Commission reassured him without neglect of their appointed tasks). Trevor Lloyd was appointed to the new Commission.

a reasoned negative case, and gently deflating the adoption of Roman Catholic practice.[39] There were other minor distractions.[40] However, the 1981-86 Commission worked largely to produce services for *Lent, Holy Week and Easter (LHWE)*. These did not disturb the authorized texts, but rather added to them. The opportunity was also used, without regard to season, to introduce an outline order for an agape within an outline (authorized) eucharist.[41]

However, during this drafting the Commission adopted some new general principles to guide their work. These not only informed their *LHWE* work, but appeared in their 'end-of-term' report, *The Worship of the Church* (GS Misc 698, 1985).[42] The new Synod debated this in November 1985, and thus guided the work of the incoming Commission. A major early decision was to extend the life of the ASB to 31 December 2000. The principles the Commission followed were:

1 The Commission needed new procedures for texts from beyond the range of 'alternatives' to rites in **1662**. Without synodical action these stood as entirely at the officiant's discretion. So the Commission began asking the Bishops to 'commend' texts for such occasions (as, e.g. in Holy Week), thus enabling new 'commended' texts (sometimes

---

[39] A couple of sentences in the conclusion give the flavour: 'the eucharist is celebrated by the whole people of God...The bishop or priest who presides... acts and speaks as the leader of the congregation...not exercising a personal power of consecration but by his presidency enabling the whole church to celebrate the memorial...'

[40] These included the House of Lords tackling a Prayer Book (Protection) Bill, and attempts in Synod to revive **S1/66**. The Lords declined the Bill, and Colin Buchanan persuaded the secretary-general of Synod that **RtB/80** permitted all in **S1/66** that anyone could want. The Commission for Covenanting proposed a rite for the reconciliation of the covenanting Churches containing the new (but odd) eucharistic prayer of the Scottish Episcopal Church. However, the Covenant itself was defeated in 1982.

[41] See *Lent – Holy Week – Easter: Services and Prayers* (CHP/Cambridge/SPCK, 1986), pp.97-98. The coaching was not repeated anywhere within the later CW range. Trevor Lloyd wrote it up in *Celebrating the Agape* (Grove Worship Booklet 93, 1985).

[42] The drafter for this initial quinquennial report was Colin Buchanan; Trevor Lloyd drafted the next three.

after airing once in Synod) to be published as quasi-official services. 'Commendation' did not enforce them as the sole rites for use, but conferred on them intangible precedence both in print and in standing as the right or best or normal Anglican way.

2 In relation to eucharistic prayers, the Legal Officer of Synod allowed that Proper Prefaces should fall within the officiant's discretion to include home-made or extemporary propers. Propers were thus exempted from the Synod's mincing-machine processes..

3 The chairman's Introduction to *LHWE* ('We are providing a *directory* from which choices may be made.') pointed the way for the Commission to produce a directory with both texts and resources such as pastoral introductions and guidelines.

4 Urban priority areas needed not just fewer and simpler words, but more expressive and pictorial imagery.[43]

5 The Commission should have closer liaison with the Doctrine Commission and the Faith and Order Advisory Group, but should be able to do its own theology without referring issues to the Doctrine Commission.

6 Most far-reaching of all, the 1981 Commission now embraced inclusive language. No longer would women have to 'love and serve all men'. The major problem, however, lay not in new drafting in the 1980s, but in living with existing hardback ASBs. Clergy and congregations were pasting in handwritten corrections, to alter what were now viewed as infelicities bordering on verbal abuse, affecting over half of the worshipping members of the Church of England.[44]

---

[43] The Archbishop's Commission on Urban Priority Areas, *Faith in the City* (CIO, December 1985), soon after asked for both language and a format which would be simpler.

[44] Some scattered advocacy of inclusive language came during the revision processes leading to the ASB. But at that stage Synod members had generally not seen the need, and, by the time it was raised, it would have been impossible to carry it as the desired policy of the Synod, and to amend all the actual texts.

The new Commission appointed in 1986 had Colin James, Bishop of Winchester, as its chairman.[45] He took with him to the Bishops David Silk and Trevor Lloyd, two of the four survivors from the previous Commission, to discuss the Commission's future work. Their paper preparing for this meeting majored on two prospective publications, one to be seasonal which in time became the seasonal resource, *The Promise of His Glory*. The other, following the policy outlined in *The Worship of the Church*, retained its 17th century title *A Directory for Worship* almost until its publication in 1989 as *Patterns for Worship: A Report by the Liturgical Commission of the General Synod of the Church of England* (GS 898, CHP) (hereafter '*Patterns*'). The Commission worked over the five years on these projects in what appeared to be a series of liturgical seminars, but the outcome would be revolutionary.[46]

The Commission also addressed the steer given by *Faith in the City* (published in December 1985), looking for both language and a format which would be simpler for the less literate to handle. In the matter of inclusive language in December 1988 they produced the report, *Making Women Visible*, which not only established principles, but also included recommendations for the minimal revision of ASB texts to solve the presenting problem, the high visibility of men.[47] They also implemented

---

[45] It was at this point that Colin Buchanan ceased to be a member.

[46] Their discussions also led to three paperback symposia, each edited by Michael Perham. The first two, *Towards Liturgy 2000* (SPCK/Alcuin, 1989) and *Liturgy for a New Century* (SPCK/Alcuin, 1991) came largely from Commission members, but through the Alcuin Club , whereas the third, *Renewal of Common Prayer: Unity and Diversity in Church of England Worship: Essays by the Liturgical Commission* (CHP, 1993) was overtly a Commission publication. Kenneth Stevenson had an essay about the eucharist in each of the first two, but otherwise the three volumes did not address it.

[47] It was not their first report. That was, somewhat surprisingly, *The Liturgical Ministry of the Deacon* (GS Misc 281, CHP, 1988), While the more catholic parts of the Church of England regularly provided a so-called deacon's role at the celebration of communion, it was without rubrical warrant and was never officially viewed as integral to the rite. In the whole revision process it was not written into the eucharistic text even as an option, until Common Worship gave it passing mention. The role was somewhat emphasized in 1987-94 when women were ordained as deacons, but could not become presbyters.

the provisions in the Canons for trial use of draft texts in selected parishes without prior exposure to the rigours of Synod.

The major creative work came from the UPA sub-group of Trevor Lloyd, Kenneth Stevenson, Jane Sinclair and Bryan Spinks. The Commission discussed their papers on issues such as: the historical relationship between the word service and the synaxis or first part of the eucharist; the structure of the eucharist and the eucharistic prayer; the nature of lectionary provision; detailed textual work on words such as 'show' and 'plead', and on the implications of this agenda for the concept of common prayer. The results of these papers and discussions emerge in summary form in the Introduction to *Patterns*. Sections on Common Prayer, Reading the Bible, Service Structure and the Eucharistic Prayer, together with the brief commentary on the Eucharistic Prayers (GS Misc 333, by Bryan Spinks and Kenneth Stevenson) provided some of the reasoning The Commission included highly imaginative material for use across the range of liturgical services: confessions, intercessions, thanksgivings, words to introduce the Peace, words for the breaking of the bread, blessings; all with rich provision for seasons and for varied secular themes, all in the shape of building-blocks which could be brought into the framework of services as appropriate. For the eucharist RtC/89 was provided in the form of skeletal headings to a structure (pp.18-20). The key distinctive feature was four highly innovative eucharistic prayers. Particularly they elided the 'first epiclesis', inserting an invocation of the Spirit following the narrative and related in different ways to the anamnesis. The Introduction called this change 'a trinitarian balance but not necessarily a trinitarian pattern' (p.13) – i.e. the Preface addresses the Father, the narrative (and the run-up to it and the anamnesis) relates to the Son, and the one epiclesis invokes the Spirit.[48] The Introduction

---

[48] The introductory 'Instructions for the Eucharist' (pp.27-29) listed the 'normal' pattern of a eucharistic prayer but did not mention a 'first epiclesis' or 'petition for consecration' preceding the narrative, even though such a paragraph was not only 'normal' but exclusively requisite in all the uses lawful in 1989! The listed pattern is on p.56 below.

also expounded a rationale of 'consecration', that it is effected 'by the whole prayer' and thus 'cannot be identified with particular words or a particular stage in the prayer', thus echoing both Lambeth 1958 and the Liturgical Commission of 1964-80.[49] The prayers also had a highly responsive nature, a wide seasonal provision, and scope for inserting 'proper' material not only as listed with two of the prayers but also in Prayer D from the great range of thanksgivings elsewhere in *Patterns*. Prayers B and C both introduced a new key verb in the epiclesis, invoking the Spirit to 'show' the bread and wine to be the body and blood of Christ.[50] Prayer C interestingly concluded with the Sanctus.[51]

Patterns as a total report was brought to Synod by Colin James for a 'take note' debate on 22 February 1990.[52] He highlighted the impossibility of providing 'sets of authorized words which were limited to a particular constituency', whether UPA, rural, family service or a particular tradition: 'what we have tried to do is to work out some patterns and principles arising out of the historic worshipping tradition...'. Amid a generally enthusiastic welcome, one episcopal voice queried various features of the eucharistic prayers, and particularly attacked the verb 'show' as 'extremely slippery and difficult'. Other members questioned the playing down of the narrative, and also the variety of wording for the narrative in the different prayers. Within general enthusiasm for *Patterns* few specifically applauded the eucharistic prayers. At the end the chairman announced that the Commission would revise the material in the light of the debate, and the Bishops would decide what material needed 'full synodical authorization'. At its March meeting the Commission worked its way through 33 written comments, set up a sub-group of Trevor Lloyd,

---

[49] See pages 13 and 25 above and the relevant footnotes on those pages.
[50] There was some small precedent for this in the Liturgy of St Basil, where the Greek verb is ἀναδεικνυμι
[51] See Bryan D Spinks, *The Sanctus in the Eucharistic Prayer* (Cambridge, 1991)
[52] A 'take note' debate means that no decisions are reached, but a subject is aired without members taking sides. In this case much content was open to the 'commending' of the Bishops (see pp.26-27 above), but specifically eucharistic texts would need full synodical authorization.

Michael Perham, Jane Sinclair, Bryan Spinks and Kenneth Stevenson to produce a complete revised text to be reviewed by the Commission in September before going to the Bishops in January as two major collections, one for authorization, the other for commendation.

The legal position was that any service which was alternative to one in the BCP had to be authorized, using the Synod's liturgical business procedure.[53] This applied to the *Patterns* outline 'A Service of the Word', alternative to Morning and Evening Prayer (together with the confessions, absolutions and Affirmations of Faith) , and to the outline RtC/89, alternative to Holy Communion (together with the eucharistic prayers).All the rest could be 'commended' by the Bishops after revision by the Commission. The Bishops agreed that 'Service of the Word' could be introduced to Synod for authorization, and this duly occurred in 1993. Its provisions included permission for it to replace the Ministry of the Word in a eucharist, which in turn allowed this part of the eucharist to be led by a deacon or reader.

In January 1992 Colin James, together with Kenneth Stevenson and Trevor Lloyd, presented the revised *Patterns* prayers to the Bishops, who, after a fairly abrasive and unsatisfactory discussion, declined to introduce them to Synod in July. Reflecting later in March, the Commission felt the Bishops' reaction was understandable 'given the sheer bulk of the material they had been presented with' but that 'they had failed to grasp the essentially restrictive and restraining aim of the proposals' in a situation where an increasing number of vibrant churches were operating outside of recognizably Anglican norms. The political decision to proceed by way of a new rite ('C') rather than revising **RtA/80** in order to avoid opening the floodgates for wholesale amendments to Rite A at this stage had also not been explained. The Commission would work on two of the four prayers, plus one for use when children were present, as

---

[53] Set out in *Patterns* p.287f

the Bishops had requested.

During 1991-94 various other issues emerged which had a bearing on the future of the eucharistic rites.[54]

The danger of losing Common Prayer: one direct result of the 1990 synod debate on *Patterns* was some extended discussion on the Commission, which noted 'there had been recurrent expressions of nervousness on the issue of common prayer' and 'doubts that adequate controls existed...' in the light of the wider range of options proposed. The *Patterns* approach enabled a discussion of the future of Anglican liturgy as a common core (authorized structures and some authorized texts) around which were gathered multiple options in text, music and action. In such a setting ancient and modern could sit side by side, as they do with hymns and music. This was worked out and tested in the Commission's dialogue with the Prayer Book Society, in an exchange of papers and meetings such as the Praxis conference on Common Prayer in 1992. Among the results of this hopefully less divisive approach were the arrival on the Commission in 1991 of Phyllis (P.D.) James, crime writer and PBS vice-president, using her English language skills to the benefit of Common Worship. There was also the publication of the Commission's papers as *The Renewal of Common Prayer* (GS Misc 412, CHP/SPCK, 1993). The need for this work had been clearly flagged up in the Commission's end of quinquenium report *The Worship of the Church as it approaches the third millennium*((CIO 1991). It was part of an ongoing debate about the identity of Anglican Worship which led among other things to the acceptance by Synod in the 'One Book or a Series of Volumes?' (GS1114) debate in July 1994 that parts of the BCP as commonly used

---

[54] Apart from the developments listed here, a private member's motion in July 1994 asked the Bishops to state the theological grounds for confining eucharistic presidency to bishops and presbyters. The Bishops amended the original motion so ask the Bishops to make a statement about 'the theology of the Eucharist and about the respective roles of clergy and laity within it'.

would be provided alongside the new CW texts, including eventually **CW/00**(OrdTwo).[55]

A eucharistic prayer for children: in 1991 Synod passed a diocesan motion from Coventry, seeking a eucharistic prayer specifically for when numbers of children were present.

Extended Communion: discussion with the Bishops led in November 1993 to a Synod 'take note' debate on the principle of 'communion by extension', with a draft by the Commission available as an 'illustration' of how this could be implemented.[56]

Language: after David Stancliffe had succeeded Colin James as Chairman in 1993, at the same time as he was becoming Bishop of Salisbury, the Commission had further discussion about language, and presented a report on 'Language and the Worship of the Church' (GS 1115) at the July 1994 Synod. This looked at different language registers, traditional and modern, and favoured mixing them (as with hymns) within a service, expressed doubts about translating traditional texts into modern language, preferring to see the Commission 'work with and as poets, to develop a vibrant and creative rhetoric which issues in memorable and prayable texts.' It re-affirmed the Commission's stance on inclusive language, looked at the possibility of a new psalter, and shared the Commission's views on the new (1988) ELLC common texts.[57]

A Service of the Word was authorized in time to be bound back up with

---

[55] In closing David Stancliffe declared that 'the whole point about Prayer Book texts is that we need to get them out of separate Prayer Book-only books such as exist if we are to get them regularly used.' This led to over 150 'traditional' pages in CW main volume.
[56] See pp.123-124 below.
[57] See the Appendix on pp.124-125 below.

all the 'commended' liturgical material, and be published as (hardback and official-looking) *Patterns for Worship* (CHP, 1995), though, of course, without the eucharistic prayers. RtC/89 as such had ceased, but, even without eucharistic texts, this *Patterns* book retained from the original 1989 five pages on 'The Eucharist: Guidance and Instructions', and the appendix of sample services provided eleven eucharistic samples and only six non-eucharistic ones.

The Commission had meanwhile worked on the eucharistic prayers, the only part of the 1989 *Patterns* following a different route to authorization. They became possible alternative eucharistic prayers to expand the range in **RtA/80**. Authorization could yet give them three or four years use before final revision would provide definitive texts for the next century.

So the Commission now brought to the Bishops in January 1994 five re-touched prayers with some family resemblances to RtC/89, but including one overtly for when children were present (EPs/94), the product of a joint Commission/Board of Education working group chaired by Trevor Lloyd. They still lacked any substantial theological or historical rationale presented in their introduction.[58] The Bishops, still being swayed by some over-cautious members. declined simply to introduce the draft prayers into Synod for authorization; they considered asking Synod whether they would like to have the prayers introduced; but even that was too bold. Instead they took the five prayers to Synod in July 1994 for a 'take note' debate followed by a fence-sitting motion:[59]

---

[58] This came five months after the international conference sponsored by IALC to do preparatory work for a full Consultation on the eucharist in 1995; and the conference became memorable for Thomas Talley's far-reaching paper on the eucharistic prayer (see David Holeton (ed), *Revision of the Eucharist* (Alcuin/GROW Joint Liturgical Study 27, Grove Books, Bramcote, 1994)).

[59] The Bishops little regarded the lapse of time. By sending their prequel resolution to Synod, and then getting a reply back, they wasted a whole session of Synod, and the final year of the Synod's quinquennium began before the revision process started. This piled up trouble, as the story duly attests.

That this Synod invite the House of Bishops to reflect further, in the light of the Synod debate, on the eucharistic proposals [set out in the Appendix to GS 1120].

The Synod was impatient of the nervousness of the Bishops (Colin Buchanan referred to their 'delicious indecision'), and vigorously rallied round an amendment which, itself further amended, called on the Bishops to introduce 'up to five prayers'.[60] The key verb 'introduce', which the Bishops had avoided, now governed procedure. The Synod then replaced the Bishops' havering motion with this clear resolution:

That this Synod invite the House of Bishops to introduce Eucharistic proposals including up to five eucharistic prayers, at least one of which should be suitable for use with children present, from the material set out in [GS 1120], with a view to their use in the Church over the next five years, and the subsequent inclusion of no more than five modern language eucharistic prayers in the revised rites of the Church of England from the year 2000.

This should have fired up the Bishops, but reluctance was still the name of their game. The House cut the prayers down to two (EPs(HB)/94), and introduced them for revision and authorization to the Synod in November 1994.[61] Neither the House nor the Commission provided any rationale – there was no account of how, although the Synod was ready for five prayers, the four had become two, nor any account of what criteria had determined the reduction.[62] Nor, of course, did the document

---

[60] The original proposed amendment was to invite the Bishops to bring 'up to four' prayers to Synod; the further amendment made it five.

[61] One of the ironies in this remarkable guillotining is that when 'up to four' had been proposed in July (see note .. above), Bishop Peter Dawes, moving the Bishops' motion, had resisted it partly because it reduced the actual five to four (and the further amending 'up to five' then nullified that part of his response). But now the Bishops proposed but two...

[62] Nor can Colin Buchanan, then a member of the House, recall any rationale in this decision-tak-

contain any discussion of the composition, meaning and structure of a eucharistic prayer. The Synod received simply two prayers. Period.

The day was saved in the short term by Trevor Lloyd, chairman of the Steering Committee. He introduced the texts in GS 1138 to Synod and explored the 'trinitarian' shape, criticized **RtA/80** as having added to the Western 'dislocation' of this pattern, and commended not only the two prayers tabled, but also by inference those excised by the Bishops.[63] The two prayers were duly committed to the Revision Committee, where Colin Buchanan was also a member.

The Revision Committee met in January 1995 under the chairmanship of Archdeacon Tim Raphael. They immediately restored all five prayers from GS1120, and during their work added a sixth, a responsive form of **RtA/80(1)** (and thus the only one with the 'Western' pattern of two epicleses).[64] They added in rubric and texts about 'The Preparation of the Gifts' and about the distribution of communion to fit the prayers consistently into RtA80 and marginally improved it. It went to Synod in July 1995 for its First Revision Stage. With Standing Orders changed since 1979, Synod members had now to propose motions to refer named items back to the Revision Committee to secure some stated change. Astonishingly, there were no motions whatsoever to remit any part of any of these six prayers back for further revision. Thus they would go unchanged to the Bishops for any final re-touching prior to voting on Final Approval. Then

---

ing. It was more that, under some vigorous chairmanship, the House could find it had taken decisions without much recollection of a debate or a vote.

[63] Trevor Lloyd at last enunciated clear principles for the Commission's 'trinitarian' shape. His speech was reproduced in *News of Liturgy* in December 1994 and is therefore available on line (via the Grove Books Ltd website). It can be compared with the Thomas Talley lecture mentioned in footnote 58 above.

[64] The Commission minutes record that the proposed increase of prayers from two to six 'had given rise to some annoyance in the HB and some reflection on the opportunities available to the House to intervene.'

they would need two-thirds majorities in each House to be authorized.

However, a hurdle stood in the way. The delays since 1992 meant that the July 1995 debate immediately preceded the dissolution of Synod. When the new Synod was elected, for internal reasons voting on Final Approval could not be taken that Autumn, so the texts went to the Bishops in both October 1995 and January 1996; and, after minimal tinkering by the Bishops, they came to Synod on 13 February 1996 to be authorized for use until 31 December 1998 – allowing just sufficient time for serious experimental use before further revision with a view to incorporation into Common Worship, which would succeed the ASB in 2000. But in Synod the texts (**95-96**) hit a disaster – newly elected members with no knowledge of the earlier stages raised objections; a few thought six too many; one or two objected to the 'trinitarian' shape of five of them; one bishop who had himself been involved in re-touching the prayers now opposed two of them;[65] and those members opposed to all modern liturgy would inevitably vote against them. In the upshot, although the Clergy were nearly 80% in favour, the Laity failed, in a vote of 135-81, to obtain the necessary two-thirds majority. The Bishops also nearly defeated their own business – 25-10 meant it would have been lost if but two had voted the other way. A project nearly ten years in formation had hit the buffers.[66]

---

[65] This was Mark Santer, Bishop of Birmingham, and co-chair of ARCIC II. He attacked prayers 1 and 3 as prejudicial to ARCIC's work, a surprising verdict from a Commission which generally ignored liturgical texts, but appealed at intervals to **1662**, and certainly could not have been embarrassed by prayers authorized as short-term 'alternatives'.

[66] Colin Buchanan and Trevor Lloyd had planned Grove Worship Booklet 136, explaining and commending the six prayers, for April 1996. In the event they had swiftly to rethink the project, and they produced a different Booklet 136, *Six Eucharistic Prayers as Proposed in 1996* (reminiscent of 'Book of Common Prayer as Proposed in 1928'). By permission this included the full six prayers and to this day it affords the easiest access to the texts. It also reproduces the Commission's guidance concerning 'Eucharists for use when Children are Present', which the Revision Committee had recommended for inclusion with the prayers in all printings of them.

5. Restart 1996-2000

The Commission met on the evening of the day the six prayers were defeated, but more time was needed for reflection, with the membership of the Commission changing, so the new Commission did not start its work until October, There were now but four years to run to complete the whole range of new rites to succeed the obsolescing ASB. The draft revision of the eucharistic rites, first discussed by the Commission in September 1995, was already in process; Michael Perham introduced the drafts to Synod in July 1996, listing the Commission's intentions:

- to have 'greater clarity of structure' where 'legitimate freedom, variety and spontaneity' were 'balanced by clear shape and structure that give both security and momentum to the liturgy.'
- to 'simplify the layout of the services and to reduce rubrics, creating a "cleaner" and less cluttered' text
- to 'make it easier for people to draw on traditional texts in contemporary language services… in accordance with the "old and new together" approach' already approved by Synod.

The Commission had originally anticipated that the **95-96** eucharistic prayers would by then be in use, and that the insights learned from their use would inform the decisions about what combination of prayers would go into the new rites. So now the pressure was on to provide new eucharistic prayers to take their place. But the Commission recognized the need for both some in-depth working with the Bishops and some kind of consultation with the Synod to convey a greater understanding of what the Commission was doing. The first was achieved through a discussion paper written by the Chairman for the Regional Groups of the Bishops, together with a closer pattern of working with the House's Theological Group. The second had to wait until July 1997 when one evening in York standing orders were suspended and the Synod was treated to a 90-minute multi-media presentation, master-minded by

Trevor Lloyd, in which most members of the Commission, together with David Hope, Archbishop of York, took part. Synod members in buzz groups answered questions like 'If you were shipwrecked on a desert island, what four items would you need in order to receive communion?' The presentation ranged from the Passover meal and 1 Corinthians 11, via slides, video clips and interviews, with side-glances at the different components and issues, 'right up to Michael Perham, chairing the Rites A and B Steering Committee, who told the Synod that it might well soon be looking at six eucharistic prayers in CW, three ASB ones revised and three new ones. Finally the buzz groups commented on the number, language and content of the prayers. The full text of the presentation and a summary of the responses were published.[67] Reflecting on this in October, the Commission noted 'the wide range of perceived needs for eucharistic prayer' and 'the wide range of understanding of the issues and comprehension of the breadth of existing practice within the church.'

Michael Perham's mention of six prayers was the first indication of developments since Autumn 1996. Even prior to this Synod discussion, when the Commission met in January 1997, the Bishops had already agreed the need for a major educational task to be undertaken before Synod discussed any draft texts. They had nominated 20 parishes in each diocese for the trial use of drafts. They had also indicated that six was the maximum number of prayers they would contemplate. They would prefer common texts for the opening dialogue, the lead-in to the Sanctus, the dominical words in the narrative and the lead-in to the final Amen. Some did not want any intrusion of responses (unless they were optional), which ruled out any responses which took the action forward. So the Bishops were engaged with the process, potentially in a fairly restrictive way, before the newer members of the Commission had had the chance to discuss what was needed, let alone formulate theological or liturgical

---

[67] For the full text and responses from Synod, see *Eucharistic prayer in the Church of England* (GS Misc 512, 1997). This was made available both for the Bishops' discussion on eucharistic prayers in October and for the Synod in November.

principles on which the new prayers could be drafted.[68] But the time was short, and the degree of mutual trust and willingness to work together on the Commission, together with a greater degree of flexibility in the Bishops and some hard work on the Revision Committees produced some good results.

'Rites A and B Revised' duly proceeded through Synod and Revision Committee, and from it the CW eucharist emerged in four separable 'Orders' – Order One being rites gathering the descendants from **RtA/80** and **RtB/80** along with new draft eucharistic prayers in both 'contemporary' and 'traditional' language, while Order Two was strictly **1662**, also in two language registers, the traditional form being **1662** itself, 'The BCP service as commonly used'.[69]

As Standing Orders forbade the reintroduction of defeated proposals, in January 1997 the Commission had agreed that Michael Perham would work (with power to draw in others) on re-working the existing **RtA/80** Prayers, and David Stancliffe would chair a varying group to work, largely by correspondence, on new drafts. James Jones, Jeremy Haselock and Christopher Cocksworth were each charged with taking advice and providing a draft for discussion in April.[70] The Commission then very thoroughly addressed and re-drafted both the existing ASB prayers and the three newly-drafted eucharistic prayers.

Other events in 1997-98 included:

---

[68] The Commission's minutes in April 1997, when the initial drafts were considered, said 'it was recognized that the need to begin drafting... soon after the January meeting ... meant that there had been no opportunity for the Commission as a whole to voice general principles before drafting began.'

[69] Quite apart from the predictable problem of reconciling different views of what 'commonly used' meant, the Commission discussed with the Legal Adviser in October 1996 potential problems with copyright if the service was simply included in CW without going through a Synodical process which made it alternative to itself. The result of this was the publication in April 1997 of GS Misc 487 'Rite B according to the pattern of the BCP'(see NOL April '97) for inclusion in the current work of the Rites A and B Revision Committee.

[70] For the detailed results of this process, see chapter 10 below.

- three attempts at Synod to discuss the Commission's draft of extended communion: it fell off the agenda, because it was not part of the time-constrained CW package. It finally achieved General Approval (with a heavy vote against) in February 1998.
- a separate treatment of the Lord's Prayer, and of the Nicene Creed [71]
- a consideration of the report commissioned by the Bishops on Eucharistic Presidency.
- In November 1997 the Commission sent six eucharistic prayers as drafts for 'trial use' under Canon B5(A) to the 800 named parishes.

The Commission received the comments of the trialling parishes in May 1998, and re-touched the six prayers to introduce them to Synod for authorization in July 1998. They gained General Approval and were remitted to their Revision Committee. Then November 1998 saw the Second Revision Stage, for 'Rites A and B Revised' and extended communion had its First Revision Stage. The six eucharistic prayers were still before their Revision Committee.

General Synod next met in July 1999. The First Revision Stage re eucharistic prayers saw a motion for a responsive prayer passed, against the advocacy of the Steering Committee.[72] A motion for the first part of the ICEL-originated prayer ('silent music') as a preface to Prayer F was accepted by the Steering Committee.

The Revision Committee on eucharistic prayers went to work and not only came up with a short, pithy, responsive (and 'Trinitarian') new prayer (which became Prayer H), but also accepted not just part but

---

[71] See David Hebblethwaite, *Liturgical Revision in the Church of England 1984-2004*, pages 41 and 24 respectively.

[72] See pp.77-81 below, and Colin Buchanan, *Prayer H – An Unauthorized Account*.

the whole of the 'silent music' text, and, after revising it, included it as Prayer G. Thus they reported at the Second Revision Stage in November 1999, and Synod accepted Prayer G, but ran into trouble with Prayer H. It was rescued by the chair of the business committee, leading Synod to suspend Standing Orders in order that, with a Third Revision Stage allowed in Synod, the Revision Committee had much better opportunity to get Prayer H right.

The Revision Committee did the requisite work, and a Third Revision Stage came in Synod on 28 February 2000. The eucharistic prayers were then approved and went to the Bishops – where they were united with the other eucharistic material in 'Rites A and B Revised'. The Bishops, meeting early on 29 February, smoothed the order of the (jumbled) material in the Preparation of the Table, and brought the unified texts, otherwise unchanged, to Synod on 1 March for Final Approval by 31-0; 175-1; 164-17 (**CW/00**OrdOne and OrdTwo). An advance text labelled 'Sample' on each page was published as a booklet for study in April 2000, and **CW/00** then went into the main Sunday Book, *Common Worship: Services and Prayers for the Church of England*, authorized from Advent Sunday 2000, just before **RtA/80** and **RtB/80** lapsed on New Year's Eve.

6. Prayers for use with children

Requests for eucharistic prayers which would be accessible to children began in the 1970s, and rumbled on until the Synod finally decided in 2006 that children could be communicant before reaching an age of confirmation. If children were to be communicant, then eucharistic prayers which included petitions for fruitful reception could be written to be accessible for such children. This became a wholly separate exercise in the years 2008-12, and the story is told in chapter 10 below.

Part 2
Thematic Treatments

7. Shape

As noted earlier, Gregory Dix injected the word 'Shape' into live use in liturgical discourse. His 'fourfold' shape was first exemplified in the CSI liturgy in 1950; and his identification of the first of the four dominical actions with the bringing of the elements to the table found expression in the 1958 Lambeth Report.[1] The Conference recommended 'The Offertory, with which the people should be definitely associated to be more closely connected with the Prayer of Consecration'.[2] A key comment on this came from Arthur Couratin, adumbrating how he (later to be the main draftsman of the Commission's eucharistic proposals) would expand their thesis:

> This is admirable – so far as it goes. But surely they might have gone further. They might have had the courage to say that Offertory, Consecration, Fraction, Communion, should be more closely associated with each other, might follow one another in a clearly defined sequence, as clearly defined as it is in the Gospels...[3]

So Dix's 'shape' was Couratin's model, and by the 1960s the Commission was agreeing Dix's shape as the groundplan for their eucharistic work.

Couratin duly brought his newly drafted eucharistic rite to the Commission in September 1964. Unsurprisingly, it mirrored his, 'Offertory, Consecration, Fraction, Communion...in a clearly defined sequence'. He also included before this sequence a greeting of peace,

---

[1] This identification of the first action is addressed in chapter 9 below.
[2] *The Lambeth Conference 1958* (SPCK, 1958) 2.81
[3] Arthur Couratin, *Lambeth and Liturgy* (Church Union pamphlet, 1959) p.9.

though without any ceremony. This followed CSI precedent, reflecting Dix's clear rationale of a reconciled and united people approaching the Lord's Table, though CSI were themselves adopting the Indian Syrian practice.[4]

Within the 'sequence', Couratin changed the titles into: 'The Preparation of the Table', 'The Thanksgiving', 'The Breaking of the Bread', and 'The Sharing of the Bread and Wine'. These untechnical titles would, he advised, help to lodge the outline shape of Dix's programme in worshippers' minds.[5]

It is the first action of the shape, the 'taking' of the bread and wine, which has proved controversial. Dix – and the bulk of the later *Parish and People* and Parish Communion devotees – identified this with the bringing of the elements to the table. The term 'offertory', though meaning the collecting of gifts in **1662**, had been easily transferred to the preparation of the elements, matching the Roman Catholic usage.[6] So this preparation became the first of the four dominical acts.[7] In Couratin's first draft, both

---

[4] Dix, *The Shape of the Liturgy* (Dacre, 1945), pp.105-108. The Syrian source of the CSI use we owe to Phillip Tovey (see L.W.Brown, *Relevant Liturgy* (SPCK, 1965) p.60).

[5] Couratin said, when introducing the draft order (S2/65) at the Liturgical Conference in February 1966:
'They say we ought to have used the proper words: the offertory, the consecration, the fraction, the communion. But we were thinking about the young confirmation candidates. There are some difficult words that these people have got to tackle...but we really did not think we need worry them with ecclesiastical words, so we tried to use something more intelligible.' (The Liturgical Conference 1966, *Report of Proceedings*, p.72)

[6] Couratin completely dismissed the **1662** meaning of 'offertory' when providing a glossary in another context:
'OFFERTORY That section of the service in which the bread and wine are brought to the celebrant. Sometimes incorrectly applied to the alms, which are also in our service brought up at the same time.' (Henry de Candole and Arthur Couratin, *Re-shaping the Eucharist* (CIO, 1964) p.41)

[7] Compare John Robinson's 1662 text for Clare College Chapel, Cambridge, in the late 1950s, which he laced with interpretative cross-headings. The 1662 offertory (still in the ante-communion) was headed '*THE FIRST ACTION: TAKING*' (John A T Robinson, *Liturgy Coming to Life*, 2nd edn, Mowbray, 1963) p.91. Dix's 'shape' had become so conventional that it was being imposed on a rite not so shaped.

actions came under a new title 'The Preparation of the Table'. The five indented rubrics disappeared from the narrative within the Thanksgiving, so that the 'taking' became an action in its own right in 'preparation', and could not be a dramatizing accompaniment to the account of Jesus 'taking' the elements and designating them his body and blood.

The demarcation of the other three actions was more straightforward. For the second action the great central prayer ('The Thanksgiving') followed, but also the opening rubric called it 'The Prayer of Consecration'. Without indented rubrics in the narrative the text allowed the theory that the whole thanksgiving consecrates; but it clearly did not compel such an understanding, as Couratin himself remained on this point an old-fashioned anglo-catholic.[8]

The third action was the Breaking of the Bread. It no longer occurred during the reading of the narrative, but was now a separate liturgical action in its own right. Its accompanying text from 1 Cor. 10.16-17 related to the unity of the people of God in the body of Christ, and tacitly excluded any suggestion that 'breaking' is a dramatization of the passion.

Finally came the Sharing of the Bread and Wine, now introduced by the Lord's Prayer and a presidential invitation, and, with the short words of distribution ('The Body of Christ', 'The Blood of Christ'), and the recipient's response of 'Amen'.

Such were the components of the Commission's draft text in 1964. In principle that 'shape' has remained throughout all subsequent revision, and has been incorporated into the texts descended from **1662** and **S1/66**. Changes in the first action are reported in chapter 9 below. But the other demarcations continue intact: a great thanksgiving as a

---

[8] Colin Buchanan's clearly recollects this in conversations with him, but also, *inter alia*, Couratin confirms it in published comment decrying the Lambeth formula of 'consecration by thanksgiving': 'The narrative identified the Church's Prayer with the Lord's, and therefore effected what the Lord himself effected – the consecration of the elements… This is the Anglican tradition, and it has good claim to be primitive.' (Arthur Couratin, *Lambeth and Liturgy* (Church Union, 1958) p.12)

single prayer; a discrete breaking of bread; and a distribution of both elements with a naming of them in delivery. Other items– such as the Lord's Prayer, Agnus Dei, an invitation and even Humble Access – have been fitted round and into this stable framework. These four actions are so self-containedly separate from each other that, as shown earlier, the Liturgical Commission and the General Synod could address creating eucharistic prayers on their own in both 1994-96 and 1998-2000 without reference to the other three actions; and, similarly, in 1996-2000 a Revision Committee of Synod worked on the other three actions without reference to the eucharistic prayers. Only at Final Approval in 2000 did the four actions become a single rite.

Dix's assertion that the early church formed and canonized this fourfold shape is seriously questioned today. Thus Bradshaw and Johnson write:

> ...it simply is not the case that all early eucharistic meals followed either a sevenfold or a fourfold shape, a view that can only be sustained by refusing to accept any testimony to the contrary. [9]

So one asks: does this verdict undermine the fourfold structuring of the eucharist followed from 1964 onwards? The answer is 'Not necessarily'. The verdict certainly removes any self-deceit that we walk exactly in the steps of 'the primitive church'. But, however strong Dix's impact, whatever Couratin's motives, or whether indeed the early centuries had any common usage, the Church of England is not bound by any such findings. It inherits a principle of producing an official eucharistic liturgy; it is committed to obey the Lord's command 'Do this in remembrance of me'; and it has scattered exemplars from two millennia of others' rites.

---

[9] Paul Bradshaw and Maxwell Johnson, *The Eucharistic Liturgies: Their Evolution and Interpretation* (Alcuin/SPCK, 2012) pp.20-21. Their own footnote refers to an article by Bryan Spinks, 'Mis-Shapen: Gregory Dix and the Four-Action Shape of the Liturgy' in *Lutheran Quarterly* 4 (1990),

But it has freedom – as the Commission and Synod have known – not to conform to any historical model. Bright ideas (and not so bright ones) have combined with the riches of tradition to provide Common Worship; and they do have a four-action shape, but not because it is commanded, nor because they follow Dix to the letter, but because, once this particular shape was adopted, it has served a pastoral purpose. So a scholarly critique of Dix has academic interest, but without prejudice to the actual eucharistic rites of today.

8. The Word, the Prayers and the Peace

The major task in this Study concerns the sacramental part of the rite, but changes in the prior parts are here briefly summarized under their **CW/00**(OrdOne) headings.

1 Opening greetings: **RtA/80** began these with a scriptural sentence, which **CW/00** dropped.

2 Collect for Purity: this continues unassailable, said congregationally.

3 Penitence: in **S3/73** this section followed the prayers. **RtA/80** allowed it either there or here (where it was printed). **CW/00**(OrdOne) has it solely at the beginning.

4 Collect, readings, sermon and Creed: these have continued with little change from S2/65.

5 Intercessions: these have continued in the same order, initially with texts within the rite, but now with a rubric suggesting topics and with sample versicles and responses.

6 Peace: **S2/67** had an (optional) verbal greeting of peace and a response, but no action. **S3/73** had the congregation stand for the greeting, and its Opening Notes offered 'a handclasp or similar action' as an option (and it was then it caught on). **RtA/80** gave a choice of presidential introductions ('*or other suitable words*'), and a rubric added '*all may exchange a sign of peace*'. *Patterns for Worship* in 1989 cited an opening note in RtA/80 allowing the Peace at different

places in the rite and *Patterns* itself offered 27 seasonal and thematic introductions. Finally **CW/00**(OrdOne) had simply '*a suitable sentence*', with seven introductions in an appendix and more under seasonal headings.

9. The Preparation of the Table and the Taking of the Bread and Wine
We come to the first action of Dix's 'fourfold' shape. Dix expounded the dominical 'taking' as fulfilled in representative lay people bringing the elements to the president, with the thanksgiving to consecrate them to follow as the second action. That to him was the 'offertory' - the 'layman's liturgy', the ritual where lay people are proactive and their actions representative. It has, in his view, nothing to do with collecting money.

Couratin followed Dix: the first action was the preparation of the table. In **S2/67** the cross-heading was 'The Preparation of the Bread and Wine', and the rubric required the elements to be placed on the table. As then authorized, the section had no spoken text, so ran into no doctrinal dangers. 'Taking' was not mentioned there, but two indented rubrics about manual acts were restored to the narrative by the Convocations. These appeared to reinstate the **1662** emphasis, that, when we say that the Lord 'took' bread and follow his cue and do the same, we then fulfil the first of the actions. This placing of the first action halfway through the second one, viz. the great thanksgiving, somewhat muddled the order which had come in cleaner form from the Commission.

S1/65, derived from **1662** and the IntrmRt, did permit the preparation of the table to come immediately before the eucharistic prayer. Collecting alms was still called the 'offertory' and it still came after the sermon and before the intercessions – but the placing of the elements on the table could come either there or after the Comfortable Words, and also could be accompanied by verses from 1 Chronicles 29, ending in 'All things come of thee, O Lord, and of thine own do we give thee.' The **1662/** IntrmRt line of descent then moved its order in the following stages:

(a) **S1-2/76** allowed the 'offerings of the people' before the intercessions, but without provision for placing elements on the table then. Both then came under 'The Preparation of the Bread and Wine' with an uncertain rubric *'The priest begins the offertory'*; the offerings of the people were mentioned next (if not collected earlier), and the bringing of the elements to the table followed and the 1 Chronicles 29 passage could be said.

(b) **RtB/80** still allowed the offerings of the people before the intercessions. Then, under the heading 'The Preparation of the Bread and Wine', came the first (unexplained) rubric *'The priest begins THE OFFERTORY'*. But then the order of **S1-2/76** was reversed, so that the placing of the elements preceded the offerings of the people, and their action now attracted 1 Chronicles 29. No separate mention of 'taking' the bread and wine occurred (in contrast to the clarity in **RtA/80**).

(c) In **CW/00**(OrdOneTrad) the earlier place of gathering the people's offerings has ceased. The sacramental action begins with a two-line cross-heading and five rubrics, all drawn from OrdOne and described on p.55 below.

By 1971, with S3/71 the Commission was clear that 'taking' was to be a separate action, and bringing elements to the table, whether by a lay procession or not, was a functional preliminary to the taking. The cross-heading 'The Taking of the Bread and Wine' introduced three rubrics in clear separation from each other:

A hymn may be sung and the offerings of the people may be collected and presented.
The bread and wine are brought to the holy table.
The president takes the bread and wine.

This pattern carefully distinguished the actions. Without indented rubrics for manual acts within the narrative, so a 'taking' to precede the 'thanksgiving' became a logical sequence. The rubrical simplicity hardly encouraged any symbolism of 'offertory processions'. However, the floor of Synod slightly blurred the message by adding to the second rubric the 1 Chronicles 29 passage, which (as it concerns gifts of substantial value) would have better gone with the first rubric. [10]

A different side-wind came from *The Presentation of the Eucharist* (SPCK, 1971), 'The report of a joint working party' of the Liturgical Commission and the Council for the Care of Churches. [11] This distinguished between preparing the elements and the presidential 'taking' of them (thus consigning Dix to history). But the report heaped symbolism into the bringing of the elements to the table – an offertory, 'the offering of our lives and the fruit of our labours to God'. [12] The working party saw this as the prime understanding of the action, a view in no way shared by the Commission itself.

This run-on from Dix (as also from Parish and People) gained momentum in the 1970s from the new Roman *missa normativa*, much favoured by some Anglicans. The Roman offertory prayers then read as follows:

(for the bread)	*(for the wine)*
Blessed are you, Lord, God of all creation. Through your goodness we have this bread to offer, which earth has given and human hands have made. It will become for us the bread of life. **Blessed be God for ever.**	Blessed are you, Lord, God of all creation. Through your goodness we have this wine to offer, fruit of the vine and work of human hands. It will become our spiritual drink. **Blessed be God for ever.**

These prayers not only had Rome's cachet, but also meshed with the

---

[10] Part of the argument in Synod was about promoting (financial) stewardship, but the amendment had been attached to the wrong rubric.

[11] The 14 members had only two from the Commission and the Commission neither saw the text in draft nor sanctioned it.

[12] *The Presentation of the Eucharist*, p.14.

symbolic understandings of some popular Anglican devotion. The Commission gave no encouragement to these texts in RtA/78, introduced into Synod in July 1978.[13] Thus submissions to the Revision Committee pressed the Committee to incorporate the Roman prayers in the revised text. Many Committee members were not inclined to Roman ways and resisted texts about offering elements to accompany the preparation. So the Committee proposed in RtA/79, for the placing of the elements on the table, a liturgical curiosity – *viz.* a congregational response without a versicle to cue it, thus:

> *The president may praise God for his gifts in appropriate words to which all respond*
> **Blessed be God for ever.**

In Synod a predictable debate arose – one vocal group wanting the Roman prayers (as printed above), and another wanting to delete the whole section, retaining the Commission's rubrical simplicity. Colin Buchanan, defensively steering the Committee's unprecedented proposal, compared it to the lingering smile of the Cheshire Cat – some observers would detect that the visible smile exactly indicated that invisibly behind it was the cat, present and welcome; while others would see some odd atmospherics, but would reckon them harmless, and go on their way. The Synod accepted the illustration in this spirit and the rubric went unchanged into **RtA/80.**[14] Under the heading 'The Preparation of the Gifts' came the placing of the elements on the table and also the 1 Chronicles 29 passage; but the 'Taking of the Bread and Cup' was a

---

[13] The text in RtA/78 did call the preparation of the table the 'offertory'. However it located the 'taking' of the elements under the separate cross-heading 'The Taking of the Bread and Cup and THE THANKSGIVING'. 'Offertory' was deleted in RtA/79; 'The Preparation of the Gifts' replaced it then; it has become 'Preparation of the Table: Taking of the Bread and Wine' in **CW**.

[14] Colin Buchanan got a letter from the Lewis Carroll Society to say that, as he had made learned reference to *Alice in Wonderland,* could they please have his text to quote.

completely distinct further section, so the preparing the table remained a preliminary before the eucharistic action began. No text encouraged 'offertory theology'.[15]

When the Commission appointed in 1986 returned to eucharistic questions, they included in the original 1989 *Patterns* some completely new ideas for preliminaries to the four-action shape, building on the Maundy Thursday service in *LHWE*:

At the eucharist we are with our crucified and risen Lord.
We know that it was not only our ancestors,
but we who were redeemed
and brought forth from bondage to freedom,
from mourning to feasting.
We know that as he was with them in the upper room
so our Lord is here with us now.
Until the kingdom of God comes
let us celebrate this feast.
Blessed are you, Lord, God of the universe,
you bring forth bread from the earth.
Blessed be God for ever.
Blessed are you, Lord, God of the universe,
you create the fruit of the vine.
Blessed be God for ever.

The passover echoes here were amplified in the Bishops' 1994 report *Eucharistic Prayers* (GS1120, Annex 1) with suggestions for question and answer preliminaries to the eucharistic prayer, spoken by children, such as 'Why do we give thanks and praise to God?', 'Why do we come to his table?'[16]

---

[15] Colin Buchanan published *The End of the Offertory* (Grove Liturgical Study 14, Grove Books, Bramcote, 1978) in June 1978. This hardly affected the revision process, but has since helped to prevent 'offertory theology' becoming assertive mainstream Anglicanism.

[16] The full texts are in Trevor Lloyd, *Children at Communion: How to involve children in the Eucha-*

Eucharistic Prayer A in *Patterns* began

We celebrate together the gifts and the grace of God.
We take this bread,
We take this wine,
to follow his example,
and obey his command.

This echoed the words at the start of the eucharistic prayer in *Eucharist for the Seventies*, giving the congregation words that took the action forward and put down a clear oral marker for one part of the four-action shape. It only disappeared from the Commission's list of Prayers at the Table in October 1998, when they needed to reduce the number of congregational prayers.

When the Commission first considered the revision of **RtA/80** and **RtB/80** in November 1995, a paper by Michael Vasey led to what the minutes described as a 'protracted discussion' on 'table prayers'. He outlined five different functions for such prayers:

- acknowledging the link with the poor (part of ancient practice)[17]
- picking up the Irenaean theme of the present Roman prayers
- receiving the people's offerings
- anticipation of the eschatological mystery
- trembling before the awesome action.

This list, and the 20 prayers then provided, indicate the size of the problem for a Commission on which a majority desired it be done in silence! The Commission wanted to avoid pre-empting the eucharistic prayer, but the stewardship lobby was pressing them to include words

---

rist, (Grove Worship Booklet 205, Grove Books, Cambridge, 2010).
[17] The General Instruction (and the current text) of the Roman Missal explicitly mention gathering goods for the poor.

about the collection, and there was pressure from anglo-catholics wanting the Roman prayers unamended, and from evangelicals who would only countenance such prayers if drastically amended.[18] Three further complications intruded: a question whether Rome would stick with 'offer' or accept the ICEL proposal of 'present before you'; the Commission's hope that the 1 Chronicles 29 text ('Yours, Lord....') and the Roman prayers might get lost in a larger selection of prayers;[19] and the curious decision to divide the prayers into congregational ones and presidential ones, the later reversal of which resulted in some good material being lost. Another strong submission from the Central Board of Finance's Stewardship Committee resulted in two more prayers about money being added. The Commission's preferred option of silence is mentioned in neither note nor rubrics, nor is there any suggestion that the prayers are limited to those in the supplementary texts: the ICEL drafters were working with 50 at one stage, so there is scope for invention!

The proposal in *Patterns* had linked the taking to the thanksgiving, and thus distanced it from the preparation of the table. The overture was missing from the prayers submitted to the Bishops in 1992 and 1994, and from the six prayers defeated in 1996; but it recurred in the family of James Jones, as Eucharistic Prayer D was prepared in 1997-98.[20] The Commission then adopted the overture text for all its Prayers. Meanwhile the Roman 'offertory' prayers, silently enabled by that unique rubric in **RtA/80**, persisted in use. So the Commission now also proposed the Roman 'offertory' prayers, but changing the controversial 'to offer' into 'to set before you'. This had been in the **1928** anamnesis, and had recurred in the Commission's original Eucharistic Prayer E which had gone for trial use, but the Commission had then corrected it to 'bringing before you'.

---

[18] In the end the Revision Committee accepted the Commission's 'set before ' as a compromise between 'offer' and 'share'.

[19] The Revision Committee admitted 'a distinct emphasis on providing variety so as to avoid over-focused and constant use of one or two particular texts.'

[20] See the text from the first draft of Prayer D on p.82 below.

However, attempts to make the prayers proposed for the preparation of the table consistent with the retouched eucharistic prayers failed.[21]

The Bishops thus received before final approval an amalgam of texts in an appendix of 'Prayers at the Preparation of the Table'. Some promoted giving money, some were from draft Prayer D as shown above, one was the famous CSI 'Be present, be present', one a text with patristic roots 'As the grain…so…may your whole church soon be gathered', and others of a general sort. The Bishops imposed a more ordered sequence, and it was authorized with the whole of **CW/00**(OrdOne). The double heading 'Preparation of the Table – Taking of the Bread and Wine' was now followed by:

A hymn may be sung.
The gifts of the people may be gathered and presented.
The table is prepared and the bread and wine are placed upon it.
One or more of the prayers at the preparation of the table may be said.
The president takes the bread and wine.

And, despite pleas on the Commission about preserving the four-action shape, the new note 17 (in the main CW Book, p.333), 'clarifying' the rubrics at this point, allowed the taking to be done during the eucharistic prayer.

17 The Taking

…The bread and wine must be taken into the president's hands and replaced upon the table either after the table has been prepared or during the Eucharistic Prayer.

So this well-hidden Note undermines the rubric in the text, allowing

---

[21] Michael Vasey, who died in June 1998, had pressed very strongly for 'set before', insisting it was uncontroversial, and therefore acceptable.

1662-type manual acts to return as the 'taking' during the narrative (i.e, halfway through the thanksgiving), and distorting the fundamental order of 'Taking – Thanking – etc'.

10. Eucharistic prayers: Origins

Amid the many eucharistic prayers, some charting of developments is needed. As a full eucharistic prayer figures second in the four-action 'shape', the prayers themselves have broadly exhibited this structure set out in the introductory section of the 1989 *Patterns for Worship*:

> An opening dialogue
> An introduction to praise
> An extended act of thanksgiving
> The narrative of institution
> The memorial prayer
> The prayer for the blessing of the Spirit
> And the concluding doxology.[22]

Over the years under review all the prayers, newly drafted or adapted from IntrmRt, moved towards this framework. Variants occurred – alternative places for a consecratory epiclesis; intercessions in **CW/00**(OrdOne) Prayers E and F; repetitive congregational responses as options following different paragraphs in some prayers; and the Sanctus as the climax in Prayer H. But the basic pattern remained close to the list above.

We identify 'families' of eucharistic prayers as follows, in their chronological order in the revision processes, not in their **CW/00** order:

(a) The 1662 line (including some 'contemporary' language forms)

---

[22] See 1989 *Patterns for Worship* (p.28). In 1989 no existing authorized eucharistic prayer conformed to this pattern.

(b) The Hippolytan descent

(c) The ICEL 'silent music' inheritance

(d) The responsive format

(e) Texts without ancestry: 'This is his story', the 'new Western' prayer, and 'The Garden of delight'

(f) The child-orientated

10(a). The 1662 line

1662 remained the sole lawful use for just over three centuries, and spread itself across the English-speaking world. It is still entrenched as a norm in law. **1928** preserved over 90% of its language (though shuffling the order), and the later fall-back, IntrmRt, even more closely preserved **1662** language.[23]   As doctrine is expressed within forms of worship, it is to **1662** that doctrinal appeals are directed.[24]   There also remain worshippers who value using **1662** (often 'done' in some favourite way). So the era of revision was bound to retain **1662**, and the somewhat undefined IntrmRt indicated how **1662**'s offspring might appear.

As noted above, after 1 May 1966 bishops retained no imagined power to make unauthorized services lawful. Now any variant on **1662** would have to attain a two-thirds majority in two Upper and two Lower Houses of the Convocations and in the Laity. Texts were needed quickly in Autumn 1965; but the Liturgical Commission declined to address editing of **1662**-type rites. So an unnamed group of bishops produced with Jasper the 'Series 1' proposals (S1/65) – marked by a slightly nervous

---

[23] For a thorough explanation of IntrmRt and of further, largely Romeward, developments from it, see Mark Dalby, *Anglican Missals and their Canons: 1549, Interim Rite and Roman* (Alcuin/ GROW Joint Liturgical Study 41, Grove Books, Cambridge, 1998). This developed his earlier study 'Alternative Services: the Canon of Series 1' in *Church Quarterly Review* (October-December 1967).

[24] This is explicit in the Canons and in the Declaration of Assent. It is to **1662** that the Anglican-Roman Catholic International Commission (ARCIC) appealed when it (somewhat late) found itself needing to cite an official liturgical text.

quest for 'the long prayer'. Chief characteristics were as follows:

(i) The Prayer of Humble Access still followed Sanctus (and Benedictus qui venit).
(ii) The prayer following was still entitled the 'Prayer of Consecration'.
(iii) The **1662** text (and indented rubrics for manual acts) ran unchanged to '...in remembrance of me'.
(iv) A rubric allowed 'Amen' then to close the prayer, or it ran on in one of two forms in parallel columns. Both columns began with an anamnesis truncated from **1928** (and sometimes used in IntrmRt texts):

> Wherefore, O Lord and heavenly Father, we thy humble servants, having in remembrance the precious death and passion of thy dear Son, his mighty resurrection and glorious ascension, entirely desire thy fatherly goodness mercifully to accept this our sacrifice of praise and thanksgiving...

Both columns reproduced wording from the **1662** post-communion prayer, sometimes dubbed the 'Prayer of Oblation'. The left column gave the whole prayer, whereas the right one eliminated its second half, and so excised the self-oblation which evangelicals had always opposed within the prayer of consecration.

The Convocations made some small changes. The title 'The Consecration' had come before 'Almighty God, our heavenly Father, who of thy great mercy', but now preceded the opening dialogue, although the rubric in the later place still called it 'the Prayer of Consecration'. And Humble Access, while still printed after Sanctus and Benedictus qui venit, had a rubric that the priest shall '*say this prayer, if it has not already been said*' – and, an earlier rubric after the penitential section, now permitted Humble Access there, referring forwards to the text printed after Sanctus as shown. The 'Prayer of Consecration' stood otherwise unchanged as far as the narrative, although the breaking of the bread could be omitted during the narrative and instead be done after the Lord's Prayer which followed the Prayer of Consecration. After the anamnesis it was the left column which (along with petitions for the departed in intercessions) led to the opposition in the Laity, where the two-thirds majority was narrowly obtained with a vote of 174-79.

S1/66 thus obtained a seven-year licence from 7 November 1966. In 1973 the renewal to December 1979 provoked less opposition, and was carried by: 23-00; 114-13; 90-25.

In the Synod debate in 1973 on 'The Future Course of Liturgical Revision' Jasper suggested bringing together **S1/66**, which was having its licence renewed, and **S2/67**, which had already had its renewal. He proposed to bring the major elements of both these existing rites as alternatives within the fourfold shape. Thus was conceived 'Series 1 & 2 Revised' (S1-2/75). It printed Humble Access after the penitence, without any mention within the Prayer of Consecration.[25] Opening Note 12 allowed that, when the **S1/66** text was being followed, the **1662** position for Humble Access could be used, and also that (as in **S1/66**) the Prayer of Consecration could end with 'Amen' following the narrative. However, after the anamnesis there were now two eucharistic prayers in parallel columns, displaying the rite's hybrid character. The left column (Prayer A) followed the **S1/66** Prayer but without its controversial longer alternative ending in the left column in **S1/66**, so the Prayer now read as a single text. Additionally, the **1662** epiclesis before the narrative gained during revision a reference to the Holy Spirit.[26] It now read:

Hear us, O merciful Father, we most humbly beseech thee; and grant

---

[25] This title remained within the rubric before the opening dialogue, but the overall title of the section was now 'The Thanksgiving', in line with the fourfold 'shape'.

[26] This conformed it to the similar addition made in **S3/73** during its passage through Synod in 1972, the amender citing the text of ARCIC I's 1971 Statement on the Eucharist. See chapter 11.(g) re the epiclesis.

that by the power of thy Holy Spirit we receiving these thy creatures of bread and wine...may be partakers of his most blessed body and blood.

. Beside it as Prayer B came the eucharistic prayer from **S2/67**, which, being from the Hippolytan descent, is considered in the next section. The unloved resultant **S1-2/76** enabled lovers of traditional language to retain the linguistic culture while moving towards the accepted Dixian 'shape'.

The questions not only recurred towards 1980; they also multiplied. For, while **1662** itself remained authoritative and vocally supported, now not only were **S1/66**, **S2/67** and **S1-2/76** to be assimilated into the more definitive programme, but also some BCP-lovers were calling for **1662** in contemporary language.

For traditional language rites **S1-2/76** could be brought into ASB format, thus providing all that devotees of **S1/66** or **S2/67** could want. These became Rite B (**RtB/80**), where Prayer A of **S1-2/76** became the First Thanksgiving (with the text now 'lined out' for presidential reading) and Prayer B the Second Thanksgiving, following it rather than being in parallel columns. **RtB/80** was duly incorporated into the ASB, and **S1/66**, **S2/67** and **S1-2/76** lapsed.

But these rites were also to be in contemporary English. The Liturgical Commission initially drafted a modern form of Prayer A from **S1-2/76** to be the Third Eucharistic Prayer in RtA/78 (without indented rubrics for manual acts, as the fourfold 'shape' made the breaking of bread a separate action). **1662** itself in contemporary language was permitted by rubric, finishing the Prayer after the narrative, and rearranging other features of the rite into the BCP order. However, in the Revision Committee the Brindley-Beckwith petition clarified what further editing was needed.[27] The Hippolytan prayer desired by Brindley became the

---

[27] See p.23 above.

Third Eucharistic Prayer and the modern form of Prayer A from **S1-2/76** became the Fourth Eucharistic Prayer. Then, following the main text, there came a new section 'The Order following the pattern of the Book of Common Prayer' (hereafter 'BCP-order'), and this used the wording from the Fourth Prayer, but from the confession onwards exactly followed **1662** without alternatives.

The ASB ran unchanged till 2000, but by 1990 the Prayer Book Society (PBS) was pressing for generous treatment of **1662**.[28] Thus, when **CW** came into view, the same **1662** and **RtB/80(A)** texts, unaltered in content and in both traditional and contemporary language, were displayed in a fuller way. The latter prayer in its **RtA/80(4)** form became Prayer C in **CW/00**(OrderOne) and also prayer C in **CW/00**(OrdOneTrad): it retained its original **1662** pattern in **CW/00**(OrdTwo and OrdTwoContmp).

Table 1 - The 1662 Family

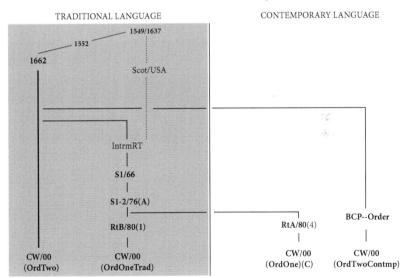

TRADITIONAL LANGUAGE — CONTEMPORARY LANGUAGE

1549/1637
1552
1662
Scot/USA
IntrmRT
S1/66
S1-2/76(A)
RtB/80(1) — RtA/80(4) — BCP--Order
CW/00 (OrdTwo) — CW/00 (OrdOneTrad) — CW/00 (OrdOne)(C) — CW/00 (OrdTwoContmp)

---

[28] See pp.32-33 above

10(b). The Hippolytan descent

R.H.Connolly concluded in 1916 that the extant 'Egyptian Church Order' was in fact the *Apostolic Tradition* of Hippolytus of Rome – a reliable witness to liturgical uses in Rome in the late second century AD.[29] Gregory Dix, in his edition in 1937, simply asserted:

> The little Greek treatise whose title is…the *Apostolic Tradition*, was put out at Rome by the anti-Pope and martyr St Hippolytus in the second decade of the third century.[30]

No ifs or buts – not only did Hippolytus describe the uses of his day, but, reporting the *paradosis*, the 'Apostolic Tradition', he also witnessed reliably to how Christians had worshipped in preceding decades. And Dix's confidence in this finding ran strongly thereafter, not least through his own reinforced advocacy in *The Shape of the Liturgy* (1945).

We call the document 'Hippolytus' here, though attributing it to an historic Hippolytus of Rome commands no comparable confidence today.[31] But Hippolytus underlies the origins and development of the new mainstream eucharistic prayers, which arose when confidence in Hippolytus was at its zenith. Those 1958 Lambeth findings, that we possess patristic evidence unknown to Cranmer (and can therefore perfect his work), almost certainly implied that Hippolytus was the major newly added source.[32] Hippolytus' influence upon the Commission's first eucharistic drafting in 1964-66 derives from the theories of the two

---

[29] R.H.Connolly, *The So-Called Egyptian Church Order and Derived Documents* (Cambridge, 1916)

[30] G.Dix, *The Apostolic Tradition* (SPCK, London, 1937), p.xi.

[31] The most thorough reversal of its status was executed by Paul Bradshaw, Maxwell Johnson and Edward Phillips in Harold W.Attridge (ed), *The Apostolic Tradition: A Commentary* (Fortress, Minneapolis, 2002). Since then Bryan Spinks has underlined that reversal: 'This document [*Apostolic Tradition*] was, in the 1960s, regarded as crucial for liturgical renewal. It has now become something of an albatross.' (*Early and Medieval Rituals of Baptism*, Ashgate, 2006, p.28).

[32] See the quotation on p.13 above.

heavyweight liturgical scholars, Ratcliff and Couratin. While Couratin provided the actual drafting, he portrayed himself as a junior colleague of the real expert, Ratcliff. Ratcliff had proposed that the Sanctus, which is not found in Hippolytus, had in fact been the climax of praise at the end of his eucharistic prayer.[33] Couratin contributed an academic proposal that the early Christians saw themselves mirroring the elders of Israel in Exodus 24, who, once sprinkled with 'the blood of the covenant', were admitted to the mountain-top to eat and drink in the presence of God.[34] Less daringly, Couratin adopted the credal sequence in Hippolytus 'Through whom...through whom...through whom...' as a good model for the Preface (unlike Hippolytus he inserted seasonal Prefaces). He added the Sanctus in its normal Western position and a 'first epiclesis' to sustain as a possible belief that reciting the narrative which follows effects consecration. Hippolytus supplied Couratin's anamnesis paragraph, in which, though Christ's 'mighty deeds' were somewhat negotiable, not negotiable was Hippolytus' main verb responding to the dominical 'Do this':

We offer unto thee this bread and this cup.

That was a given – a core text of the early church. But whether it was what Jesus had actually commanded was patient of further enquiry.

After the anamnesis Hippolytus became less visible. Thanksgiving for the worshippers being found worthy to stand before God and minister to him figured lightly in this first draft; but Hippolytus' epiclesis (calling the Spirit upon the 'oblation') would have disrupted a Westernized text.[35]

---

[33] See A.H.Couratin and D.H.Tripp (eds), *E.C.Ratcliff: Liturgical Studies* (SPCK, 1976) pp.31-34.

[34] See, e.g. his 'The Sacrifice of Praise' in *Theology* (Vol.58, no 22) pp.285-291, or his 'The Thanksgiving of the People Of God' in David M.Paton (ed), *The Parish Communion Today* (SPCK, 1962) pp.52-53.

[35] The Latin text of Hippolytus calls the Spirit down upon the elements (see *The Apostolic Tradition*, p.9); but Dix, who generally follows the Latin, here downgrades the Latin text and defends this in his introductory treatment of the textual materials (*id*, p.xvii) and in an extensive end-note

Exodus 24 faintly echoed in 'we pray thee to accept this our duty and service on high in the presence of thy divine majesty'.

The Commission honed this first draft between September 1964 and September 1965; when the 'Draft Order' (S2/65) was forwarded to the archbishops for publication in December. The original 'all-sufficient sacrifice' was now 'his saving passion, his resurrection from the dead and his glorious ascension into heaven'; similarly 'looking for his coming in glory' was now 'looking for the coming of his kingdom'.[36] There were then changes between December 1965 (S2/65) and March 1966 (S2/66): the repetitive 'through whom' of the Preface was now (through Michael Ramsey's advocacy at the February Liturgical Conference) 'through him...through him...through him...'; and after the anamnesis the petition to accept our 'duty and service' became a prayer for fruitful reception, requesting that we might eat and drink in God's presence (Couratin's eye being on the elders in Exodus 24).

When Colin Buchanan dissented from 'we offer unto thee this bread and this cup', a year of debate and negotiation ensued, and it became (following **1549**) 'we make the memorial of his saving passion...'. Couratin saw his Hippolytan text damaged beyond recognition, and Ratcliff's death in June 1967 dispirited him, and the Laity's acceptance of 'make the memorial' in July finished him. He resigned from the Commission

---

(*id*, pp.77-79). The Cuming and ICEL translations of Hippolytus unhesitatingly include the invocation of the Spirit.

[36] This change was precipitated by an interchange on the Commission more or less as follows:

> *Bishop Mervyn Stockwood*: Mr Chairman, do we have to say 'looking for his coming in glory'? Would it not be preferable to look for the coming of his kingdom?
>
> *COB*: But all the early texts which have an eschatological perspective look for Jesus' coming in person in glory.
>
> *Mervyn Stockwood*: Oh, I know all you Tyndale Hall men - out in the garden with your telescopes looking for the second coming.
>
> *COB*: Well, I find it very odd that in the diocese of Southwark the kingdom can come but the king mustn't.

Southwark prevailed in the short term (see also Michael-de-la-Noy, *Mervyn Stockwood: A Lonely Life* (Mowbray, 1996) p.145).

and went into opposition. In the next 33 years the revision of this prayer never again entailed revisiting Hippolytus – from Hippolytus the prayer might have come, but to Hippolytus it was not going to return. Echoes of 'opened wide his arms on the cross', 'revealed the resurrection' and 'counted us worthy to stand in your presence and serve you' occurred in later drafting, not only in prayers of the Hippolytan descent; but the normal refining of the text was based on the perceived usefulness of proposals, and, equally, the offering of the elements to God ostensibly to obey Jesus' command never reappeared.

Further stages are simple to record. This, the one agreed prayer in **S2/67**, retained its primacy thereafter, even though re-touched *in via*. When contemporary language came, it was the sole prayer in **S3/73**; and in the further revision of 1978-79, though more prayers were added, this became 'The First Eucharistic Prayer'. It came later in a responsive form within **1995-96** prayers which the Synod rejected.[37] Then in 1997-99 it passed into Eucharistic Prayer A in **CW/00**. The Hippolytan genes were somewhat diluted, but the stud book since 1965 testified clearly to the descent.

How, then, did the wording develop from **S2/67** to **RtA/80**? As far as the narrative little was changed.[38] But in the anamnesis, acclamations, and petition for fruitful reception (the 'second epiclesis') every word was under scrutiny.

---

[37] It figured as the only one of the six prayers continuous with **RtA/80** ones, providing not new text, but a responsive form of **RtA/80**(A) already widely in use.

[38] See chapter 11 (a)-(e) below for further examination of these.

S2/67	S3/71	S3/73	RtA/78	Rta/80
'...remembrance of me.'	'...remembrance of me.' Christ has died; Christ is risen; In Christ shall all be made alive.[39]	'...remembrance of me.' Christ has died; Christ is risen; Christ will come again.	'...remembrance of me.'	'...remembrance of me.' Christ has died;[41] Christ is risen; Christ will come again.
Wherefore, O Lord, with this bread and this cup we make the memorial of his saving passion, his resurrection from the dead, and his glorious ascension into heaven, and we look for the coming of his kingdom;	Therefore, heavenly Father, we do this in remembrance of him: with this bread and this cup we celebrate his perfect sacrifice made once for all upon the cross; we proclaim his resurrection from the dead and his ascension into heaven; and we look for the fullness of his coming in glory.	Therefore, heavenly Father, with this bread and this cup we do this in remembrance of him: we celebrate and proclaim his perfect sacrifice made once for all upon the cross, his resurrection from the dead, and his ascension into heaven; and we look for his coming in glory.	Therefore, heavenly Father, we do this in remembrance of him: we proclaim his offering of himself made once for all upon the cross, his mighty resurrection and glorious ascension; and, as we celebrate his one perfect sacrifice with this bread and this cup, we look for his coming in glory. Christ has died;[40] Christ is risen; Christ will come again.	Therefore, heavenly Father, we remember his offering of himself made once for all upon the cross, and proclaim his mighty resurrection and glorious ascension. As we look for his coming in glory, we celebrate with this bread and this cup his one perfect sacrifice,
and we pray thee to accept this our duty and service, and grant that we may so eat and drink these holy things in the presence of thy divine majesty, that we may be filled with thy grace and heavenly blessing;	Accept this our sacrifice of thanks and praise; and as we eat and drink these holy gifts in the presence of your divine majesty, renew us by your Spirit, inspire us with your love, and unite us in the body of your Son, Jesus Christ our Lord.	Accept through him, our great high priest, this our sacrifice of thanks and praise; and as we eat and drink these holy gifts in the presence of your divine majesty, renew us by your Spirit, inspire us with your love, and unite us in the body of your Son, Jesus Christ our Lord.	Accept through him, our great high priest, this our sacrifice of thanks and praise; and as we eat and drink these holy gifts in the presence of your divine majesty, renew us by your Spirit, inspire us with your love, and unite us in the body of your Son, Jesus Christ our Lord.	Accept through him, our great high priest, this our sacrifice of thanks and praise; and as we eat and drink these holy gifts in the presence of your divine majesty, renew us by your Spirit, inspire us with your love, and unite us in the body of your Son, Jesus Christ our Lord.[42]
Through the same Christ our Lord;...	With him...	Through him...	Through him...	Through him...

[39] Acclamations first appeared in 1971, but that text avoided the second coming (possibly because of 'South Bank' theology). Synod ironed out both the third Acclamation and the 'fullness of his coming' lower down (see the next column), not least through Donald Coggan.

[40] The oddity of the congregation anticipating the president's anamnesis inspired this re-location of the acclamations. However, the Revision Committee thought better of it, and the later place had to await **CW** texts. See also note 41 below concerning a bidding to introduce the acclamations.

[41] In RtA/79 the Revision Committee proposed a bidding, viz 'Together we affirm our faith'. Brian Brindley then persuaded the Synod to accept the Roman 'Let us proclaim the mystery of faith', but the Synod also moved it into the opening notes, so it is absent from this text.

[42] This paragraph had had a complex history in Synod. The threefold active transitive verbs in the imperative 'renew...inspire...and unite...' had in **S3/73** in contemporary English vividly contrasted with **S2/67** 'grant that we may be filled...' But in the Revision Committee George Timms sought a petition that we might become 'a living temple' – and by a narrow majority the Committee substituted 'may we who are nourished by his body and blood grow into his likeness...and become a living temple to your glory' and proposed it thus in RtA/79(1). However, in full Synod Ronald Jasper himself proposed from the floor to restore 'renew...inspire...and unite...' (attributing it to Colin Buchanan, who, while steering the debate, asked David Silk to defend this particular text). Jasper's proposal unsurprisingly carried the Synod; but a fall-back amendment transposed the 'living temple' text to the Second Prayer, and it thus became **RTA/80**(2); see note 45 below. 'Living temple' also had a later history – see p. 76 and note 59 below.

Some key points emerged in this revision process. Firstly, the Commission was determined to supersede the stopgap text in **S2/67** 'make the memorial' – not only because of its theological ambiguities, but also because in popular speech 'memorial' suggested a tribute to the dead, rather than an engagement with the living. So the Commission resisted the Bishops' attempt in early 1978 to revert to 'make the memorial' and prevailed both there and in Synod.[43] However much juggling occurred in the anamnesis during revision, the main verb 'to celebrate' remained central. The 'looking for his coming' was also secure, and, very interestingly, to begin the petition for fruitful reception which followed, 'sacrifice of praise and thanksgiving' was introduced; it was also modified by 'accept through him, our great high priest' – for this precluded any understanding of the 'sacrifice of praise' as being the sacrifice of Christ himself. His one sacrifice, alone among all sacrifices, was immediate, and could not have been offered by his own mediation. This sacrifice was the 'fruit of lips, giving praise to his name' (Heb.13.16).

However, the story has ramifications. When **S3/73** moved the archetype **S2/67** into contemporary language, some parishes, having taken to **S2/67** (perhaps still using traditional music settings), were unwilling to be catapulted by Synod into contemporary language; and the rumour arose that this text (with 'make the memorial') was the true 'catholic' rite. Jasper met this by proposing 'Series 1 & 2 Revised' (**S1-2/76(1-2)**), which brought traditional language rites into the fourfold 'shape'. As noted in section 10(a) above this contained both **S1/66** and **S2/67** eucharistic prayers; and this latter thus gained new authorization within the hybrid rite. That was not the end of its story.

The Commission from 1976 onwards was told that, although the **S2/67** eucharistic prayer was thought more 'catholic' than the **S3/73** one, yet not all who preferred it were wedded to its language and many wanted it in contemporary speech. The Commission provided the kind of wording

---

[43] See p.22 above.

required in the Second Eucharistic Prayer in the proposed RtA/78 text. There the acclamations were followed by the **S2/67** anamnesis somewhat adjusted:

Therefore, Lord and heavenly Father,
having in remembrance his death once for all upon the cross,
his resurrection from the dead,
and his ascension into heaven,
and looking for the coming of his kingdom,
we make with this bread and this cup
the memorial of Christ your Son our Lord.

The key **S2/67** elements retained were 'looking for the coming of his kingdom' and 'make …the memorial' - the 1960s stopgaps, frozen in content, but placed within the contemporary rite.[44]

Once proposed, the text went through Synod with little debate, and became **RtA/80(2)**.[45]   However, two distant offspring texts from Hippolytus, i.e. **RtA/80**(1) and **RtA/80**(2), did not suffice. A further proposal was to come.

The Revision Committee for RtA/78 in Autumn 1978 included Brian Brindley, a knowledgeable and determined anglo-catholic. He proposed (along with Roger Beckwith, as explained earlier) a new alternative eucharistic prayer, from the Hippolytan stud-book but descending via the

---

[44] The line 'his death once for all upon the cross' stemmed from David Silk, the leading anglo-catholic in the revision process. He asserted that different churchmanships feel affirmed when they hear certain words – as, eg, anglo-catholics like to hear 'offer' and 'saints'. He insisted that evangelicals should hear what he took to be their shibboleth, 'once for all'. It could hardly be resisted; and so it went in. But in reality everyone's death is 'once for all' (Heb.9.27)! Evangelicals actually asserted that it was Christ's *sacrifice* (which distinguishes his death from all other mortalities) which was 'once for all'.

[45] The one unexpected feature of it was the insertion of the 'living temple' imagery (see note 42 above). The Steering Committee fall-back, when this was removed from the First Prayer, was include in the Second 'nourish us…that we may grow…and…become a living temple to your glory.' 'Nourish' was a concept much loved by David Silk; 'living temple' by George Timms.

Roman Catholic Prayer II of 1970, rather than **S2/67**. Its Preface echoed Hippolytus more strongly than ('born of the blessed Virgin', 'opened his arms on the cross' and 'revealed the resurrection'). Its first epiclesis, lacking Hippolytan precedent, drew from Rome. Its anamnesis followed RtA/78 texts, including a juxtaposition in 'we celebrate this memorial'. Hippolytus also echoed in: 'we thank you for counting us worthy to stand in your presence and serve you'; in a carefully crafted 'we bring before you this bread and this cup'; and, originating from Hippolytus's 'send the Holy Spirit upon the offering of your Church', came its adaptation '...on all that your Church sets before you.'

The Revision Committee havered before accepting 'we bring before you', and rejecting '... on all that your Church sets before you'. To ask for the Spirit to be sent upon the elements cut too many theological corners; and the Committee imaginatively redirected the petition '...upon your people', thus leading naturally into a petition for fruitful reception. The Synod accepted the Prayer, with only one side-battle.[46]   And so this more obviously Hippolytan text joined the existing two as the Third Eucharistic Prayer in **RtA/80**.

The Prayer caught the parochial imagination. Although all concerned wanted all texts authorized to be usable in good conscience by all congregations, this Third Prayer was deemed the pukka 'catholic' one. Many parishes used it alone, and, when parish printings were allowed, their customized booklets contained solely the Third Prayer. Indeed the Second Prayer, brought in by the Commission in 1978 to meet those who thought it properly 'catholic', was probably itself then eclipsed by the Third Prayer, which outbid its favoured role.

Eucharistic prayers in the 1989 *Patterns* and those derived from them (ie RtC/89 – Eps/HB/94) disregarded Hippolytus. As in **RtA/80** Hippolytus had already fathered three of the four eucharistic prayers, a

---

[46] The Brindley proposal, accepted by the Revision Committee, was that the first epiclesis should invoke the 'holy word' rather than the Spirit. Synod accepted an amendment to substitute 'by the power of your Holy Spirit' by a vote of 97-96.

new range was needed. Nevertheless, the Revision Committee in 1995, following the 1978 precedent of adding a new prayer during revision, both revived the prayers the Bishops had removed and also slipped in **RtA/80(1)** now adapted for greater congregational participation. This duly perished with the others in February 1996 and appears on the chart as a cul-de-sac – but the idea of a truly responsive prayer had lodged in many minds.

After 1996 preparing texts for Common Worship entailed revisiting the three Hippolytan prayers in **RtA/80**. As they closely resembled each other, the Commission decided to reduce their number by assimilating **RtA/80(1)** and **RtA/80(2)** into a single prayer. As far as the narrative the two were virtually identical, apart from the useful permission to shorten the preface in **(2)**, now switched to **(1)**; and from the 'second epiclesis' onwards the two prayers were mainly distinguished by **RtA/80(2)**'s inclusion of the 'living temple' (switched from RtA/79(1) in 1979). This phrase was now ditched altogether.[47] There remained the anamnesis, where, as shown above, **RtA/80(2)** had retained the stopgap 'make the memorial' from **S2/67**, and **RtA/80(1)** had gone beyond it with 'we celebrate…'. However the Commission now disregarded the earlier theological and literary concerns crafted into **S3/73** and **RtA(1)**; and so **CW/00(A)** lost the developed anamnesis (notably including 'we celebrate…his sacrifice' and 'looking for his coming in glory') and reverted to 'make the memorial' and 'looking for the coming of the kingdom'. These interim texts of 1967 had been preserved in **RtA(2)**, and they had been little used, for the new Third Prayer **(RtA/80(3))** had seduced the anticipated adherents. Nevertheless, now in 1998 combining **RtA/80(1)** and **RtA/80(2)** by replacing two main features of the anamnesis of RtA/80(1) with two historic survivors of **RtA/80(2)** arguably lost sight of the origins of the two texts concerned.[48]

---

[47] It proved not to have been ditched irretrievably – see p.76 and note 59 below.
[48] See p.19 above. Colin Buchanan attempted in Synod in 1999 to restore the main 1980 text, but the Steering Committee resisted this and persuaded the Synod.

The Third Prayer itself underwent some shuffling of words in the anamnesis in becoming **CW/00(OrdOne)(B)**.

RtA/80(3)	CW/00(OrdOne)(B)
And so, Father, calling to mind his death on the cross, his perfect sacrifice made once for the sins of all men,	And so, Father, calling to mind his death on the cross, his perfect sacrifice made once for the sins of the whole world,
rejoicing at his mighty resurrection and glorious ascension,	rejoicing at his mighty resurrection and glorious ascension,
and looking for his coming in glory,	and looking for his coming in glory,
we celebrate this memorial of our redemption.	we celebrate this memorial of our redemption.
We thank you for counting us worthy to stand in your presence and serve you;	As we offer you this sacrifice of praise and thanksgiving,
we bring before you this bread and this cup.	we bring before you this bread and this cup
We pray you to accept this our duty and service, a spiritual sacrifice of praise and thanksgiving.	and we thank you for counting us worthy to stand in your presence and serve you;
Send the Holy Spirit upon your people	Send the Holy Spirit on your people
and gather into one in your kingdom…	and gather into one in your kingdom…

Table 2 - The Hippolytan Descent

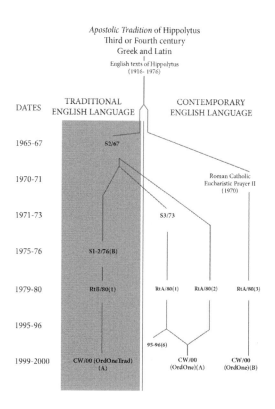

10(c). The ICEL 'silent music' inheritance

ICEL has for 50 years submitted English-language translations of authorized Latin liturgical texts to the Vatican for approval, and originally also promoted the ecumenical work on common texts.[49] However,

---

[49] See pp.124-125.

ICEL has also composed liturgical forms *de novo*, overtly for study only. And their *An Original Eucharistic Prayer: Text 1* (ICEL, 1984) came the Church of England's way. It quickly became widely known for its phrase 'all your works echo the silent music of your praise' and for drafting a feminine-like attribute of God in:

> As a mother tenderly gathers her children,
> you embraced a people as your own.

The Liturgical Commission welcomed its vivid poetic and pictorial language, and Kenneth Stevenson adapted it as the second eucharistic prayer in RtC/89. At that stage there was added a set of twelve three-line thematic insertions for use at three points in the prayer (see the table below).[50]   It then ran the gauntlet of the synodical process for ten years to emerge, a healthy survivor, as Prayer G in **CW/00**(OrdOne).

Its steps as a survivor ran as follows:

(a) Published in *Patterns for Worship* (1989) (RtC/89)
(b) Debated as such in General Synod in 1990
(c) Submitted to the Bishops in January 1992, and there remitted back to the Commission
(d) Submitted again to the Bishops in January 1994 (Eps/94(4)), and included in the House's question to the Synod in July 1994 (when the Synod asked for texts to be introduced)
(e) Survived the Bishops' reducing from five prayers to two (Eps/94HB(2)), being second of the two brought for general consideration in November 1994
(f) Remitted to Revision Committee for consideration in 1995 and

---

[50] The third insertion in each set introduced intercession in the last section of the prayer, which the Commission recognized might be a problem with some.

then returned, almost untouched, to the Synod in July (Eps/96(2)).
(g) When Synod sought no reference back in July 1995, the Bishops approved the text in January 1996; but the Synod then defeated it within the six eucharistic prayers in February 1996.
(h) Though those defeated texts were not to be re-introduced for authorization in Synod, Richard Harries proposed to the Revision Committee in 1999 that part of this prayer should form a Preface.
(i) The Committee hesitated, and clearly thought that Synod did not want more prayers, but they printed its text in Appendix 2 of their report.[51]
(j) At the Revision Stage in Synod Richard Harries moved to refer it back to incorporate part of it within Prayer E. This time the Committee re-touched and reinstated the whole prayer, now as Prayer G.[52]
(k) Prayer G was then authorized by Synod on 1 March 2000 as CW/00(OrdOne)(G).

In the table below the ICEL text is on the left, the 1989 *Patterns* text in the centre, and the authorized **CW/00**(OrdOne)(G) on the right. At some points (not least the Hippolytan 'He opened wide his arms on the cross') Prayer G has reverted to the original ICEL text. The slight variants made between 1989 and 1999 are shown by footnotes; otherwise all changes shown on the right came in 1999-2000.

---

[51] See GS1299Y, pp.10 and 48-49.
[52] They also sought a legal opinion about reintroducing; and the fine judgment was that, as they had amended the text, it was not the defeated prayer which they were introducing.

AN ORIGINAL EUCHARISTIC PRAYER – ICEL 1984	ALTERNATIVE EUCHARISTIC PRAYER B – in RtC/89	PRAYER G in **CW/00**(OrdOne)
[Standard opening dialogue, then -]	[Standard opening dialogue, then -]	[Standard opening dialogue, then -]
Blessed are you, strong and faithful God. All your works, the height and the depth, echo the silent music of your praise. In the beginning your Word summoned light; night withdrew and creation dawned. As ages passed unseen, waters gathered on the face of the earth and life appeared. When the times had at last grown full and earth had ripened in abundance, you created in your image humankind, the crown of all creation. You gave us breath and speech, that all the living might find a voice to sing your praise. So now, with all the powers of heaven and earth, We chant the ageless hymn of your glory: **Holy, holy...Hosanna in the highest. Blessed is he...Hosanna in the highest.** How wonderful the work of your hands, O Lord! As a mother tenderly gathers her children, you embraced a people as your own and filled them with longing for a peace that would last and for a justice that would never fail. Through countless generations your people hungered for the bread of freedom. From them you raised up Jesus, the living bread, in whom ancient hungers were satisfied. He healed the sick, though he himself would suffer; he offered life for sinners, yet death would hunt him down. With a love stronger than death, he opened wide his arms and surrendered his spirit, Father, let your Holy Spirit move in power over us and over our earthly gifts of bread and wine, that they may become the body and blood of Christ. On the night before he met with death, Jesus came to table with those he loved. He took bread and praised you, God of all creation; he broke the bread among his disciples and said: Take this, all of you, and eat it; this is my body which will be given up for you. When supper was ended, he poured a final cup of wine and blessed you, God of all creation; he passed the cup among his disciples and said: Take this, all of you and drink from it; this is the cup of my blood, the blood of the new and everlasting covenant; it will be shed for you and for all so that sins may be forgiven. Do this in memory of me.	Blessed are you, Lord God, our light and our salvation; to you be glory and praise for ever! From the beginning you have created all things and all your works echo the silent music of your praise. In the fullness of time you made us in your image, the crown of all creation.[53] You give us breath and speech that with all the powers of heaven we may find a voice to sing your praise: **Holy, holy...Hosanna in the highest. Blessed is he...Hosanna in the highest.** How wonderful the work of your hands, O Lord! As a mother tenderly gathers her children, you embraced a people as your own... *[Insertions (a) optional here]* From them you raised up Jesus, our Saviour, born of Mary,[54] to be the living bread, in whom all our hungers are satisfied... *[Insertions (b) optional here]* On the night before he suffered on the cross, he came to table[55] with his friends, he took bread, saying, Take this, all of you, and eat. This is my body which will be given up for you. After supper, he took the cup, and, giving thanks, he said: Take this, all of you, and drink my blood of the new covenant, shed for you and for all, that sins may be forgiven.	Blessed are you, Lord God, our light and our salvation; to you be glory and praise for ever! From the beginning you have created all things and all your works echo the silent music of your praise. In the fullness of time you made us in your image,. the crown of all creation. You give us breath and speech, that with angels and archangels and all the powers of heaven we may find a voice to sing your praise: **Holy, holy...Hosanna in the highest. Blessed is he...Hosanna in the highest.** How wonderful the work of your hands, O Lord! As a mother tenderly gathers her children, you embraced a people as your own. When they turned away and rebelled your love remained steadfast. From them you raised up Jesus our Saviour, born of Mary, to be the living bread, in whom all our hungers are satisfied. He offered his life for sinners and with a love stronger than death he opened wide his arms on the cross. On the night before he died, He came to supper with his friends and, taking bread, he gave you thanks, He broke it and gave it to them, saying: Take, eat; this is my body which is given for you; do this in remembrance of me. At the end of supper, taking the cup of wine, he gave you thanks, and said: Drink this, all of you: this is my blood of the new covenant, which is shed for you and for many for the forgiveness of sins. Do this, as often as you drink it, in remembrance of me.

---

[53] **1995-96**: in your image, the crown of all creation] in your image to reflect your glory
[54] **1995-96**: born of Mary]OMIT
[55] The narrative was changed in wording and order in 1994, introducing 'he broke it', altering 'which will be given up', and adding 'Do this in remembrance'.

Let us proclaim the mystery of faith:		Great is the mystery of faith:[56]
Christ has died...come again.	**Christ has died...come again.**	**Christ has died...come again.**
Dying you destroyed...come in glory		**Dying you destroyed...come in glory**
When we eat ...until you come in glory.		**When we eat ...you come in glory.**
Lord, by your cross...of the world.		**Lord, by your cross...of the world.**
Father,	Father, as we plead with confidence his	Father, we plead with confidence
we commemorate Jesus, your Son,	sacrifice made once for all,	his sacrifice made once for all upon the
as we offer you his sacrifice.		cross;[57]
Death could not bind him, for you raised	We remember his dying and rising in glory,	we remember his dying and rising in
him up in the Spirit of holiness	and we rejoice that he prays for us at your right	glory,
and exalted him as Lord of creation.	hand;	and we rejoice that he intercedes for us at
May his coming in glory find us		your right hand;
ever-watchful in prayer,		
strong in love,		Pour out your Holy Spirit as we bring
and faithful to the breaking of the bread.	Pour out your Holy Spirit over us and these	before you
	gifts	these gifts of your creation,
Rejoicing in the Holy Spirit,	which we bring before you from your own	may they be for us the body and blood of
your whole Church offers thanks and praise	creation;	your dear Son.[58]
together with N., our Pope,	Show them to be for us the body and blood of	As we eat and drink these holy things in
N., our bishop,	your dear Son.	your presence,
and all whose lives bring hope to this world.		form us in the likeness of Christ,
Lord of the living and the dead,	[*Insertions (c) optional here*]	and build us into a living temple to your
awaken to the undying light of pardon and		glory.[59]
peace		
those fallen asleep in faith,		[Remember. Lord, your Church in every
and those who have died alone , unloved,		land.
and unmourned.		reveal her unity, guard her faith,
Gather them all into communion		and preserve her in peace...]
with Mary, the Mother of Jesus,		
and with all your saints.		Bring us at the last with [*N and*] all the
Then, at last, will all creation be one		saints
and all divisions healed,		to the vision of that eternal splendour
and we shall join in singing your praise		for which you have created us;
through your Son, Jesus Christ.		through Jesus Christ, our Lord,
Through him,	Through him, with him, and in him,	by whom, with whom, and in whom,
all glory, strength and power are yours,	with all who stand before you in earth and	with all who stand before you in earth
Father of mercies,	heaven,	and heaven,
in the unity of the Holy Spirit	we worship you, Father almighty,	we worship you, Father almighty,
for ever and ever.	in songs of everlasting praise:	in songs of everlasting praise:
Amen.	**Blessing and honour and glory and power**	**Blessing and honour and glory and**
	be yours for ever and ever. Amen.	**power**
		be yours for ever and ever. Amen.

[56] 'Great is the mystery of faith' began in 1994.

[57] 'upon the cross' began in 1994.

[58] In this paragraph 'over us and these gifts' and 'Show them' were both omitted in 1996.

[59] Kenneth Stevenson had submitted that this imagery should be restored in Prayer A, where it had once lodged, and the Revision Committee resisted this and incorporated it in Prayer G.

10(d). The responsive ethos

The only congregational responses within the sacramental part of the 1662-type services were in the opening dialogue and the Sanctus (which was recited or sung corporately following custom rather than rubric). The compilers of 1950 CSI liturgy, with an eye to the Liturgy of St James (the major use of the Indian Syrian Churches), introduced further congregational responses, one after the narrative, the other after the epiclesis. Yet in England the eucharistic prayers of **S1/66** and **S2/67** were still presidential monologues. Congregational responses were aired in an unofficial rite of St Mark's-in-the-Bowerie in New York in 1964-65, publicized in England by John Robinson, and from the *ballon d'essai* of Trevor Lloyd and Christopher Byworth, *Eucharist for the Seventies*, in 1968. Ronald Jasper became an observer at Rome from 1966 and monitored moves there; and the *missa normative* in 1969 provided four eucharistic prayers, each with a choice of four 'memorial acclamations' following the narrative.[60] Our own Commission, working on a single eucharistic prayer for 1971, incorporated Rome's first acclamations following the Liturgy of St James: 'Christ has died; Christ is risen; Christ will come again.' The Commission initially demurred at 'Christ will come again' and substituted 'In Christ shall all be made alive' but Synod boldly reverted to the original.[61] The responsive element was increased by a crescendo-type final doxology (from Rev.5.14):

**Blessing and honour and glory and power
be yours for ever and ever. Amen.**

The Commission planned in the revision of **S3/73** to keep the acclamations ('Christ has died...etc') immediately after the narrative

---

[60] Leslie Brown, erstwhile secretary of the CSI liturgy committee, liked to think that Rome copied acclamations from CSI. It is not clear that he had any evidence (beyond mere chronological order) of such dependence.

[61] See p.66 and note 39 above.

in all the main eucharistic prayers (ie which thus brought in the Brindley-Beckwith proposal), but to keep the extended doxology only in the First Prayer. There were no increasing congregational responses in **S1-2/76** or **RtB/80**. However, the Commission recognized a need and proposed to the Bishops in early 1978 a prayer providing a recurrent congregational response through the prayer.[62]   It could also be used without the responses in contexts such as hospital chapels which had little expectation of responses. It was called a 'mini-canon' because of its brevity. The Bishops turned it down, though ambiguously deeming it appropriate for years ahead, but not yet.[63]   Thus the four eucharistic prayers in **RtA/80** simply retained the acclamations in **S3/73** with the congregational doxology solely in **RtA/80(1)**.

Patterns made further attempts in RtC/89. Prayer A had an extended introductory dialogue, a quasi-Sanctus (actually drawn from Revelation), alternative acclamations after a brief anamnesis, a congregational epiclesis, and an actual Sanctus as its conclusion. Prayer C had five brief congregational responses during the Prayer and also concluded with the Sanctus; and Prayer D had a congregational Sanctus, acclamations and doxology with much less presidential monologue than in the **RtA/80** prayers. In the succeeding interplay between the Bishops and the Commission Prayer A survived almost unchanged until July 1994; it was omitted from the two prayers the Bishops sent to Synod in November 1994; it was restored by the Revision Committee in January 1995 to become Prayer 3 in the six brought to General Synod in July 1995, among which Prayer 6 was an adaptation of **RtA/80(1)** to make it highly responsive. But these prayers were defeated in February 1996.

After this defeat, when the Commission addressed creating

---

[62] The text as proposed later in the year to the Revision Committee is published in *News of Liturgy* no.51 (March 1979) (available on line via Grove Books Ltd).
[63] Curiously the Revision Committee, while rejecting its responsive form, accepted it shorn of the responses within an appendix as 'A Eucharistic Prayer for Use with the Sick', and Synod accepted this as part of **RtA/80** (see ASB, pp.171-2). But it had fled the category of 'responsive' prayers.

new eucharistic prayers, the previously discerned need for strongly congregational responsive texts was forgotten. Their proposed Prayers A, B and C were little changed from the **RtA/80** prayers in this respect; Prayer D had its two-line interjectory following the cue 'This is his/ our story' with '**this is our song: hosanna in the highest**'; Prayer E was much as Prayer A; and Prayer F had, strictly as an option, '**Amen, Lord, we believe**' and variants on it, at up to seven points in the post-narrative text. Colin Buchanan and Trevor Lloyd both asked the Revision Committee for a prayer with substantial congregational responses with actual content to them. The Committee delivered a blunt *non volumus*:

§18. [After comment on the desire to alleviate the 'presidential monologue'] The Committee realize that the concern for congregational participation has three aspects; there is a significant number [who want no congregational intervention beyond the opening dialogue and the Sanctus]; there are those asking for regular intervention by congregational acclamation (as a repeated memorable phrase so that there is no need for texts to be closely followed[64]); and there are those who wish to see significant sections of the prayer, even whole paragraphs, presented for corporate recitation so that congregational speaking would 'carry forward' the sense and content of the prayer.

§19.The Committee returned to this issue...It has, however, not made provision for corporate speaking of substantive paragraphs in any prayer...the alternation between text spoken by one voice and corporate speaking is an essential part of the flow... particularly focussed in the Eucharistic Prayer which is, *par excellence*, in the

---

[64] This 'no need...to be closely followed' reflects an emphasis articulated by David Stancliffe and other Commission members, urging that worshippers should not be expected to read texts, but crucially to hear them. This underlying principle probably inspired the Revision Committee's further §19 which follows above. The Synod, however, would give the congregation a chance.

unbroken tradition, assigned to the presiding minister.[65]

Colin Buchanan tabled a motion in July 1999 to refer the issue back to the Revision Committee. In his speech he compared the responses in the existing prayers (not least the repetitive one-line ones) to

> Pentecostal circles where…at intervals you say 'Praise the Lord', and the congregation comes back with 'Alleluia'. You are reassured then that they are all present and listening and you can get back to what is still basically a monologue. These Eucharistic Prayers [i.e A-F] have that characteristic of a set 'Hear, hear' at intervals, 'We agree, keep going'.

Bishop David Stancliffe, chairing the Steering Committee, resisted from the platform the proposed reference back. He listed existing versicles and responses, the existing use of the Sanctus, even silence, as ways in which congregational participation was already provided. The Synod was not persuaded, and carried by 180-143 the reference back 'for further revision of the responsive material'. The reluctant Committee then took the point - with both hands. Even before Synod finished in York a draft, short, responsive prayer was circulated for informal comment. This enabled the congregation to move forward the content of the prayer (and also made the Sanctus the final doxology). Then in September the Committee sat with the written submissions and also oral evidence from some attending the Committee in person; and a new text was available during the Autumn.

The second Revision Stage in Synod was more complicated. Colin Buchanan and another member of Synod, David Bird, had submitted different sets of amendments to meet different ideas of the prayer's

---

[65] The report of the Revision Committee (GS 1299Y) pp.8-9. By 'alternation' the Committee clearly means 'monologue punctuated by one-line responses'.

purpose. As set out on a line-by-line basis in the order paper, the proposals ran a serious risk that Synod, by voting on that basis, might produce a dog's breakfast from the differing texts of the would-be amenders. The business committee saved the day; standing orders were suspended; a third Revision Stage was agreed; and the text was referred back to the Revision Committee to hear the would-be amenders in a more rounded way.

The resultant text came to the specially arranged Third Revision Stage on 28 February 2000, and no amendments were made. It received the final *imprimatur* from the Bishops on 29 February, and was then authorized with the rest of Orders One and Two by the whole Synod on 1 March 2000.[66]   It passed into widespread use.

10(e). The virtually new
(i) 'This is his story'

The defeat of the six prayers in February 1996 came as a new Commission was to appointed. Among the newcomers was James Jones, then Bishop of Hull, who had long and varied experience of all-age worship. The Commission looked to him to draft a eucharistic prayer which would clearly be child-friendly. His own preferred adjective was 'all-age'. He drafted from experience of holding informal eucharists in his home with his own children (aged 8-12) participating, and they assisted in creating a prayer in a previously untried register. In introducing the prayer to the Commission in April 1997 he indicated the elements which had guided his drafting: the importance of narrative action...avoidance of too many abstract concepts...drafting in short clauses and sentences.... brevity ...engaging the congregation in responses which were triggered by a repeating cue phrase. Taking a wide view of his brief, he also drafted

---

[66] Colin Buchanan wrote up the story in 'Eucharistic Prayer H: an unauthorized account' in *Ushaw Library Bulletin and Liturgical Review* no.13 in September 2000, and then with permission offprinted the article as a pamphlet under the same title. Charles Read gave a Revision Committee view in 'No way to run a railway' in *Anvil*, Vo. 17, no.4 (2000) pp.259-269.

forms to accompany the preparation of the table.

The first draft of his prayer became public in November 1997, when the Commission issued drafts of Prayers A-F for trial use in 800 named parishes before the authorization process began. Prayer D began then with these preliminaries attached:

HYMN   *During this hymn the children may follow those bringing the gifts and gather round the holy table.*

These words may be used at the Preparation of the Table
President   Jesus Christ welcomes to this celebration all the children of his kingdom on earth

Adults or children may present the bread and wine, and say

With this bread that we bring
All   **We shall remember Jesus.**

With this wine that we bring
All   **We shall remember Jesus.**

A *minister*   Bread for his body,
wine for his blood,
gifts from God to his table we bring.
All   **We shall remember Jesus.**

The bread and the wine are placed on the holy table.

THE EUCHARISTIC PRAYER [The prayer itself was largely as the final Prayer D]

The preliminary material passed at the next stage to the 'Preparation of the Table' in **CW/00**(OrdOne) for use with any eucharistic prayer.[67] But its origins were as part of the ethos of Prayer D.

The main characteristics of the prayer itself were there from the start, the most notable being the adaptation of the chorus of Fanny Crosby's 19th century mission hymn 'Blessed assurance' (clearly well known to James Jones' family[68]):

This is my story: this is my song
praising my Saviour all the day long.

The prayer interposed 'This is his story' in the first two occurrences, where the story of Jesus was the theme. Then it became 'This is our story', and to both cues the congregation responded 'This is our song: Hosanna in the highest'. In the trial use of November 1997 the prayer reached its climax with this same couplet; but the Commission then pruned the conclusion and sent the prayer to Synod climaxing with 'Blessing and honour and glory ...etc'. The statistical response from the trial period suggested a very mixed reaction, but some parishes may well have been quite responsibly trying a eucharistic prayer of a *genre* which was simply distant from their expectations or tastes.

Other distinctive features were: a vivid emphasis upon Jesus' incarnate ministry on earth; a straight use of 'celebrate the cross on which he died'; and an epiclesis in the Eastern position after the anamnesis, but, like Prayer C, with an invocation of the Spirit upon the communicants rather than the elements. The initial draft of this epiclesis referred to 'his body as broken bread, wine outpoured as his blood', but the text sent to Synod

---

[67] See Common Worship main volume p.292.
[68] A rumour arose that the song was unknown to the Commission's chair, David Stancliffe, whose favoured religious music was of a different *genre*, and that he therefore accepted the proposal simply for itself. During the writing of this Study he has confirmed the rumour as true.

changed this to 'with opened eyes and hearts on fire.'[69] The Synod welcomed the text and remitted it to the Revision Committee, within which James Jones was member of the Steering Committee. Some would-be amenders sent in minor suggestions, one or two disliking the chorus and one or two others suggesting it was too long or too difficult for children. One question was whether God should be called 'Good Father', but James Jones was adamant – of itself, 'father' raised hurtful associations to some children, and the added 'good' was a necessary corrective. But text had general approval, not needing revision. At the Revision Stage in Synod only one proposal was continued: Colin Buchanan wanted the verb to 'plead' (in Prayers D and E) to be reconsidered. James Jones from the platform resisted this and carried the Synod.

Thus Prayer D avoided any tampering in Synod and stood with the other seven for Final Approval on 1 March 2000. Despite its original conception, it was never overtly categorized as for 'when children are present'; and, when prayers thus designated were written, Prayer D was not identified as having already met that need. Nevertheless, it was for such a role that many parishes brought it into use.

(ii) The new 'Western' Prayer

Prayer E is the sole 'Western' prayer among the new ones within **CW/00**. Although newly created, it nevertheless draws upon the order and wording of the Hippolytan prayers. Its draft form in 1997 had a long preface (with optional one-line versicle-and-response interventions), though the expectation was that an 'extended preface' would replace it for main seasons. The trial use brought the Commission to a different mind. Now GS1299 provided in Prayer E merely a skeletal framework for the 'extended prefaces', leaving a minimal fixed preface on other occasions.[70]

---

[69] 'Broken bread and wine outpoured' reappeared in Prayer E instead.
[70] There are just 44 words joining the opening dialogue to the Sanctus

Adding such prefaces acquired free rein by a rubric: '*Here the president leads the thanksgiving for God's mighty acts in creation and redemption. This form or another suitable form must be used.*' Clearly the extended prefaces were coming along (some 'examples' were in an appendix), but the '*suitable*' here was indeterminate, apparently chartering home-made texts.

Little else was changed after the trial use; in the anamnesis 'We set before you [the bread and cup]' became 'Bringing before you [the bread and cup], we proclaim…'; but the 'Western' epiclesis invoked the Holy Spirit 'upon us and upon these gifts', departing from previously agreed texts, and, arguably, from Church of England norms.[71] Objections to this in Synod left the Revision Committee unmoved, stating 'the phrasing is precisely the same as in [*95-96(2)*]'.[72] So at the First Revision Stage in July 1999, Synod received the prayer well in general, but Colin Buchanan moved to re-commit the epiclesis to the Committee, for their report was misrepresenting the 1996 text — the Revision Committee in 1995 had specifically altered it. So Synod returned Prayer E to the Revision Committee.[73] Then in November 1999 the Committee tabled a more mainstream epiclesis '…send your Holy Spirit, that broken bread and wine outpoured may be for us the body and blood.' The phrase 'broken bread and wine outpoured', which might now rank as its signature, had come from the draft of Prayer D.[74] The phrase is vivid and arresting, but is it warranted?[75]

---

[71] See the more detailed discussion of the text of epiclesis in chapter 11.(g) below.

[72] GS1299Y, p.22.

[73] In the table on p.76 the 1995 change in the epiclesis can be seen by comparing the centre and right columns.

[74] See pp.83-84 above.

[75] The purist might note that, whereas the breaking of the bread is a dominical act, the pouring of wine is not. One may well infer that pouring figured within the Last Supper, not only from the character of a meal with different rounds of wine, but also from Jesus' words that his blood was 'poured out for many' (Matt.26.28; Mark 14.24). But the temptation to balance 'breaking' with 'pouring' has no basis in the original accounts. The text thus lurks near to a 'dramatization' concept of communion, seeing the breaking and pouring as portraying, in the actual action effected with

Prayer E has been welcomed in parishes which follow Western patterns, not least in the ceremonial accompanying the narrative, but also in using Proper Prefaces. Such parishes tend to discount Prayers D,F,G and H, in which the epiclesis comes two paragraphs *after* the narrative, and throws doubt upon any Western understanding that the narrative effects the consecration. Prayer E thus became the one new prayer that adherents of a Western view have easily adopted.

(iii) The 'Garden of delight'

Although Prayer F had no Church of England antecedents, Paul Bradshaw traces other sources for its ideas.[76]   The patristic model particularly noted is the Liturgy of St Basil, as this not only begins the story of salvation with the eternal nature of God (living in light inaccessible), but also portrays the next steps – the creation, the first humans living in innocence in God's paradise, and the fall. ICEL had done a version of St Basil (for study, as with the 'Silent Music' prayer, not with expectation that Rome would authorize it). Some echoes of Basil came in Eucharistic Prayer IV in the Roman Rite and in Eucharistic Prayer D in the 1979 Book of The Episcopal Church (USA); but nothing comparable had surfaced in the Church of England. Prayer F draws directly on St Basil (not on Rome or TEC) for its most distinctive phrase – almost its signature – 'You…placed us in the garden of your delight', a clear (and very close) revival of the Basiline phrase τεθεικας αὐτον ἐν παραδεισῳ της τρυφης.[77]   The Prayer further counts as Eastern in its 'Trinitarian' shape with but one epiclesis, its strong eschatological emphasis, and its provision, after the epiclesis,

---

the symbol, the death of Christ. Overall the Church of England's texts have steered clear of this concept – see also chapter… below on the breaking of the bread.

[76]   Paul Bradshaw (ed), *Companion to Common Worship* Vol. I (Alcuin/SPCK, 2001) p.141

[77]   In Basil the phrase comes in the post-Sanctus section, and is translated as 'paradise of pleasure' by Jasper and Cuming . Τρυφη is found in the New Testament in Luke 7.25 and 2 Peter 2.13 (where the verb is used also), in both of which occurrences it means effete or self-indulgent pleasures; but the word is lifted by its context here to portray the truly paradisal from which the effete is fallen.

of three lines of intercession. Christopher Cocksworth, who had a major part in shaping the prayer, added in an internal Commission document that the influence of St Basil emerges in 'the provision of short responses ("Amen Lord, we believe") running throughout the prayer and bringing a sense of energy, engagement and movement familiar in both Eastern and Charismatic worship.' It also has a latterday emphasis, in praying that the outcome of sharing communion may be to form the participants into a 'perfect offering'. It was hardly re-touched by the Commission after the trial period or by the Revision Committee en route through Synod.

10(f). Prayers for use with children – featuring a question and answer
The liturgical revision in the Roman Catholic Church delivered three eucharistic prayers designed for use with children. Their ICEL translation into English came from 1973. Thus a category of eucharistic prayers never previously considered now came onto anglo-catholic agendas. The Revision Committee for Rite A in 1978-79 first encountered such requests.

The Commission and the Revision Committee were both unimpressed. At root a Roman Catholic rationale differing from an Anglican one lay behind the authorization of the prayers. Roman Catholic usage did not necessitate there being lay communicants: a mass in, say, a primary school would be fully valid with its own justification, even if only the priest communicated. In addition, first communion has been widely practised in the Church of Rome from seven onwards, so that there might indeed be child communicants at such a service. Anglicans have always affirmed more that the rite was essentially for the worshippers to receive the elements, and thus the eucharistic prayer's petition for fruitful reception has no point of reference if those present are non-communicant. From 1968 onwards questions arose about the age and qualifications for children to receive communion in the Church of England; and the then prevailing requirement of confirmation (at, say, 12 or upwards) meant that few, if any, below that age would communicate. Writing eucharistic prayers for primary school children to understand would be writing for non-communicants, a somewhat paradoxical task. Admitting children to communion on the basis of their baptism before confirmation was debated in the Church of England from 1971 to 2006.[78]

No concessions were made in 1978-79. The request was viewed as partisan; and the ASB contained no eucharistic liturgy which could be labelled as 'child-friendly'. But the atmosphere was changing during the 1980s, and the Bishops in 1986 asked the Commission to provide structures and text for authorization 'alongside ASB' to include '"family" services and worship in UPAs'.[79] The Board of Education Report *Children in the Way* (NS/CHP, 1988) also recommended that:

The Board of Education and the Liturgical Commission should examine the need for new liturgies to serve all-age worship, and in particular for a form of the Eucharist suitable for when children are present. There should be full consultation...[80]

The Synod debate on *Children in the Way* reinforced this with a call for a 'shorter eucharistic prayer for use with children'.[81] There were also questions asked in General Synod. The Commission responded with its 'Rite C' proposed eucharistic prayers, fresh in brevity, flexibility and vivid concrete imagery. However, neither in the Introduction nor in association with the prayers did the Commission name 'children' as part of the prayers' rationale. They wrote:

We believe it is not right to publish prayers for this specific need

---

[78] Lambeth 1968 had raised the issue, but 1971 identifies the Ely' report, *Christian Initiation: Birth and Growth in the Christian Society* (CIO, 1971), the first official advocacy of a much younger age for admission to communion (one prior to confirmation). For an overview of the whole 35-year struggle see Colin Buchanan, *Taking the Long View* (CHP, 2006) pp.52-68.

[79] *Patterns* (1989), p.v

[80] *Children in the Way*, chapter 4 recommendation 3 (p.53), cited by *Patterns* on p.vi.

[81] Reported in *Patterns* p.11.

until such time as larger numbers of children are actually receiving communion.[82]

However, they recognized that children were often present and the language ought to be 'capable of being understood by the whole family at worship'.

The next step was the diocesan motion from Coventry. Molly Dow moved in General Synod in November 1991:

That this Synod, welcoming the initiative taken by other Churches, request the House of Bishops as soon as possible to introduce proposals for a Eucharistic Prayer suitable for use in the Church of England at services with children present.

Synod amended this to 'Eucharistic Prayers', then passed it. The Bishops duly sent the request to the Commission, but the five Prayers brought to the Bishops in January 1994 and then to the Synod debate in July 1994 in GS1120 included none overtly labelled for use with children. The Synod motion then asked the Bishops to introduce 'up to five Eucharistic Prayers, at least one...for use with children present'. The Bishops reduced the Prayers to two to go to Synod in November 1994, and added a note saying neither was 'for use when children were present'; these went to the Revision Committee which then brought six prayers to the Synod including one for use when children were present (though not quite so labelled); this allowed locally written prefaces to be incorporated into a skeletal framework; and an annex to GS1120 headed 'Eucharists when Children are Present: Pastoral Issues and Suggestions' was recommended by the Committee for publication with the Prayers; however, the whole project was lost again in the wholesale defeat of February 1996.[83]

---

[82] *Patterns*, pp.11-12
[83] See pp.36-37 above. The texts are in our *Six Eucharistic Prayers as Proposed in 1996* (Grove Worship 136, 1996).

In November 1996 the Bishops brought to Synod guidelines for admitting unconfirmed children to communion, and the Synod supported them overwhelmingly. The Bishops confirmed their guidelines and issued them in April 1997.[84]   However, this did not of itself impact the drafting of eucharistic prayers – irrespective of Prayer D's origin and character and Prayer E's, none of the **CW** prayers on which the Commission was working was placarded as 'for use when children are present'. That lack led David Bird first to press the need to the Revision Committee in 1998-99, and then, when they took no action, to attempt to redraft Prayer H for this purpose at the Second Revision Stage. Prayer H, as responsive, met one element within his submission, but without being labelled as 'for use when children are present'.

The Synod regulation in 2006 officially permitted admission to communion of children baptized yet unconfirmed, and the quest for a eucharistic prayer for use with children was renewed. Durham diocese passed a resolution, which came to General Synod in February 2008. After a minor amendment the Synod resolved:

That this Synod request the House of Bishops to commission the expeditious preparation of Eucharistic Prayers suitable for use on occasions when a significant number of children are present or when it is otherwise pastorally appropriate to meet the needs of children present.

The Bishops passed this to the Liturgical Commission, and the Commission brought two innovative draft texts to the Bishops in December 2008. The Bishops' comments led to re-touched texts being submitted to the Bishops in December 2009, and they then began a pre-synodical trial use. Both prayers sought brevity and simplicity of

---

[84] As a matter of history, the Bishops were taking liberties with the Canons, and canonical respect-ability only came with the Synod's Regulations under Canon B15A in 2004-6. See Colin Buchanan, *Taking the Long View*, pp.66-68.

language within a traditional framework. They differed in that Prayer One had an 'Eastern' epiclesis following the anamnesis, and Prayer Two a 'Western' invocation before the narrative. Other smaller distinctivenesses were that Prayer One had a triple repetition of 'Holy, holy, holy' early in the prayer, and similarly 'Amen, amen, amen' at the end – with notes suggesting a rising articulation for each threesome. Prayer Two drew upon the original passover query 'What do you mean by this service?' This was originally drafted for three different places:

> *Question (by a chosen individual or group):* 'Why is it right to give thanks and praise?'
> *Answer (by another chosen person or group):* 'Because God is love and does wonderful things'.

> *Question (by a chosen individual or group):* 'Why do we share this bread and wine?'
> *Answer (by another chosen person or group):* 'Because Jesus makes them signs of his love.'

> *Question (by a chosen individual or group):* 'Why do we follow Jesus Christ?'
> *Answer (by another chosen person or group):* 'Because he is God's saving love.'

The trial period ran from January to June 2010. The questionnaire returns led the Commission to retouch the prayers; the Bishops in December 2010 gave the go-ahead; and they came in GS 1822 to General Synod in July 2011 for General Approval. With them was (in GS Misc 983), the Commission's 'Guidance Notes for the Planning of a Eucharist at which a significant number of children are present'.

This trial period prompted one noteworthy change. In Prayer Two the three questions remained as above, but in GS 1822 in July 2011 the answers had given way to but one answer, whichever question was asked: 'Listen and you will hear'. While at least one complaint about this change came in Synod, the Revision Committee merely tweaked it to read 'Listen and we will hear'. No part of the texts was resubmitted to the Revision Committee in February 2012; the Bishops left them unchanged; Final Approval for use came in July 2012 by votes of 26-0: 110-0: 95-5. They were published with the Notes and 'Guidance on Celebrating the Eucharist with Children' in a yellow booklet in the **CW** format.

11. The structure of the Eucharistic prayer.

The structure set out on p.56 above provides the order followed here, though some sections there are sub-divided for closer consideration here. How then was each section handled in revision?

(a) The opening dialogue (Sursum corda)

1662 had no initial salutation, but all other texts from the IntrmRt onwards have had one. The traditional language form has remained untouched; contemporary forms have shown variation.

Traditional	ICET	S3/73	ELLC	CW/00(OrdOne)
The Lord be with you **And with thy spirit**	The Lord be with you **And also with you.**	The Lord is here[85] **His Spirit is with us.** [ASB *or* The Lord be with you **And also with you.**]	The Lord be with you **And also with you.**	The Lord be with you **And also with you.** *or* The Lord is here **His Spirit is with us**
Lift up your hearts **We lift them up unto the Lord**	Lift up your hearts **We lift them to the Lord**	Lift up your hearts **We lift them to the Lord.**	Lift up your hearts **We lift them to the Lord.**	Lift up your hearts **We lift them to the Lord.**
Let us give thanks to our Lord God **It is meet and right so to do.**	Let us give thanks to the Lord our God. **It is right to give him thanks and praise.**	Let us give thanks to the Lord our God. **It is right to give him thanks and praise.**	Let us give thanks to the Lord our God. **It is right to give our thanks and praise.**	Let us give thanks to the Lord our God. **It is right to give thanks and praise.**

---

[85] The authorship is unknown, but it is probably attributable to Ronald Jasper in preparing the draft text, S3/71. Geoffrey Cuming's rendering of S2/67 into contemporary language in 1968 took a liberty with 'The Spirit of the Lord be with you; **And also with you.**'

(b) Prefaces and Proper Prefaces

Western rites have traditionally provided proper prefaces for the different seasons. **1662** in a restrained way continued the practice and so have its descendants. The **S2/67** Hippolytan text followed it also (though *Apostolic Tradition* has an invariable preface), and **CW/00**(OrdOne) (E)) advertises its own Western ethos by providing proper prefaces.

A new development was that *Patterns* in 1989 proposed for use with Prayer D lengthy thanksgivings for each high season. These were held back while the Bishops hesitated over introducing new eucharistic prayers into Synod; but the six prayers finally proposed by the Revision Committee in 1995 went some way towards variety. In Prayer 1, short extemporary lines of praise could be inserted; in Prayer 2 seasonal insertions came not in the preface but at three later points; in Prayer 3 ordinary proper prefaces were indicated; in Prayers 4 and 6 none was ordered; in Prayer 5 complete liberty for home-grown texts was allowed (an appendix provided 'examples', but this child-friendly prayer gave freedom for personal or group initiatives). All perished in the defeat of February 1996.

In **CW/00**(OrdOne), Prayers D, F, G and H followed Eastern precedent with fixed prefaces. Prayers A, B, C and E followed the Western precedent of propers; but, harking back to the thanksgivings in *Patterns*, A, B and E permitted a range of 'Extended Prefaces' for high seasons. These were: Advent (two texts), Christmas, Epiphany, Presentation of Christ in the Temple, Lent, Annunciation, Passiontide, Maundy Thursday, Easter, Ascension Day, Ascensiontide, Day of Pentecost, Trinity Sunday, All Saints' Day, Kingdom Season, Day of Christ the King, Saints' Days (general).

(c) Sanctus and Benedictus qui venit

The Sanctus text proposed by ICET in 1970 was incorporated into S3/71, and, as ICET and ELLC have proposed no changes, it has lasted through all revisions unchanged. Its place as a climax to the preface has also continued unchanged in all the prayers, except drafts A and C in the original 1989 *Patterns*, and the ultimate Prayer H in 2000.[86] These exceptions reflected the Ratcliff theory that the Sanctus originally formed the climax to the whole prayer, and in them Sanctus formed the final doxology. The Benedictus qui venit, which followed Sanctus in Sarum and **1549**, was omitted by Cranmer in **1552**.[87] It was recovered by anglo-catholics in the 19th century, perhaps with the revival of Marbeck's setting for the **1549** text; but probably also with a sense that, if Rome were using it, it properly belonged with Sanctus, whether sung or not. It was almost automatically printed in versions of the IntrmRt, and was added in square brackets in S1/66. **S2/67** made it a separate (optional) anthem printed after the eucharistic prayer; it disappeared in **S3/71** and **S3/73**, but returned within RtA/78, now as an option immediately following Sanctus. **RtA/80** entrenched this, though understandably not in the BCP-Order. It has followed Sanctus as an option in all eucharistic prayers since, save in strict **1662** texts and the three with Sanctus at the end.[88]

(d) The link to the narrative

From the mini-climax of the angels' song the structure of a eucharistic prayer requires a 'link' to lead to the narrative, the invariable warrant for each eucharistic celebration. In 'Western' prayers the wording has to incorporate en route a 'first epiclesis'; in Eastern ones it leads directly to the narrative.

---

[86] In the ASB the 'Eucharistic Prayer for use with the Sick' in an appendix omitted Sanctus altogether (in the interests of total length, but also with no necessary expectation of a vocal congregation joining in).

[87] See the discussion in Colin Buchanan, *What did Cranmer think he was doing?* (Grove Liturgical Study 7, Grove Books, Bramcote, 1976 and 1982), p.27.

[88] There is a careful discussion of the text in the ELLC booklet, *Praying Together* (Canterbury Press, 1990) pp.23-24. Requests had been made that, for inclusive language, the translation should read 'Blessed is the one who comes...', but ELLC insists that the quotation from Psalm 118.26a refers specifically to Jesus, and the masculine form is appropriate.

In **1662**, and thus in **CW/00**(OrdTwo or OrdTwoContmp), the link was a new start after the Prayer of Humble Access. It also incorporated the doctrinal undergirding of the eucharist: 'who made there [ie on the cross] (by his one oblation of himself once offered) a full, perfect and sufficient sacrifice, oblation and satisfaction for the sins of the whole world'. Latterday adaptations of **1662** via the IntrmRt have retained this wording here, even though a restored anamnesis has later allowed further doctrinal content to be included. Prayers of other ancestries sometimes refer to Jesus' example and command, and some 'Eastern' ones reflect briefly on Jesus' eternal nature and his incarnation. But in essence the paragraph is a single sentence, its purpose to bring us to the Last Supper.

(e) The narrative of institution – text and role

An account of Jesus' Last Supper, with his command to his disciples to 'do this in remembrance of me', is known here as 'the narrative'. Traditionally it has led on from the preface and Sanctus to provide a warrant for the current celebration. In the Sarum rite which Cranmer inherited, it crucially provided the formulae deemed to consecrate the elements, viz, Jesus' words 'This is my body', 'This is my blood'. This understanding was retained less prominently in **1549**; but in **1552** the remaining two manual acts disappeared and no objective consecration of the elements remained. The narrative's role was simply adjectivally to provide the warrant in the command 'Do this in remembrance of me'. After **1559** a concept of consecration slowly reasserted itself until **1662** provided five manual acts by rubrics indented into the narrative. Consecration by 'This is my body/blood' was established, and other rubrics carefully distinguished between consecrated and unconsecrated elements.[89]

---

[89] There is a clear difference between what effects consecration and what consecration effects. In **1662** the liturgical question as to what effects consecration was answered with words and manual acts comparable to Roman Catholic use; but the dogmatic question as to what consecration effects was answered in accordance with the Elizabethan Settlement, rather than the decrees of the Council of Trent.

In **1662** the narrative was an adjectival subordinate clause, introduced by the relative 'who' grammatically within a larger sentence. Apart from minimal variation to make its language contemporary, the same wording continued through all revisions and in all eucharistic prayers until 1980 (partly because the bishops, as itinerants, wanted to recite the same narrative without recourse to a book).[90] The same text of the narrative survived in CW in the descendants of **1662, RtA/80,** and **RtB/80.** **CW/00**(OrdOne) had no indented rubrics concerning manual acts, but the 1662 five rubrics recurred in full in **CW/00**(OrdTwo).

This verbal conformity disappeared with new drafts after 1980. *Patterns* set a style in RtC/89. Each Prayer stood as a narrative with main verbs in no subordinate role; and each Prayer had now its own uniquely worded narrative, echoing the style and thought-form of the prayer. So the shortest prayer (RtC/89(D)) had the shortest narrative, even lacking the dominical command.[91]

The reasoning behind this was to reflect the different ways of handling the narrative in the New Testament and in catholic history, and to avoid exalting the narrative in a way that would appear to favour one particular view of consecration. The comparatively detached view of the narrative, in both the *Patterns* sub-group and the Commission, is reflected in the way the Commission discussed in principle whether to have one prayer without the narrative. The Commission contented itself in the end with saying 'In the continuing debate on the development of the eucharistic

---

[90] The only attempt to vary the text was Geoffrey Cuming's amendment to substitute 'for' for 'who' as the lead-in to the narrative. This in the context of **S3/73** and **RtA/80 (1)** would have made the narrative slightly more obviously the warrant for the current celebration, rather than being simply information tacked on adjectivally to the previous sentence. Geoffrey Cuming lost by 117-116 in February 1979, and, returning in July to try it on the Second Eucharistic Prayer, he lost by 85-82.
[91] On the night before he died
Your Son Jesus Christ took bread and wine.
He gave thanks and said
This is my body, given for you.
This is my blood, shed for forgiveness of sins.

prayer the narrative is regarded as a later insertion.'[92]

A question persists about presidential actions during the narrative's recitation. Rubrics about manual acts had in **1662** identified a point of consecration, but they were dropped entirely from **S3/73** and in all prayers thereafter, except in the **RtA/80** BCP-order and in **CW/00**(OrdTwo). Nevertheless the recent 'Western' Prayers (i.e. **CW/00(A)**, **(B)**, **(C)**, **(E)** and Prayer Two of the Additional Prayers) still allow such a doctrine of consecration through the dominical words, even though the omission of indented rubrics and manual acts has discouraged that view. The 'Eastern' Prayers (i.e. **CW/00 (D)**, **(F)**, **(G)**, **(H)** and Prayer One of the Additional Prayers) seem to exclude such a doctrinal understanding of the narrative's role, as in them the epiclesis calling for the Holy Spirit to imbue the action follows after the narrative and anamnesis. This makes little sense if the elements have already been consecrated during the narrative. Parishes with a 'Western' understanding of consecration often set these Prayers aside.

Overall, from the first suggestion in the Lambeth 1958 Report there has been a hesitant transition to seeing consecration as effected by the thanksgiving character of the whole prayer. The narrative has been an integral feature of the prayer, but not as providing 'moments' of consecration for the elements. Manual acts may still be found, though the point is well made if they are not. The change does not imply an 'Eastern' type epiclesis must be identified as providing a different 'moment' of consecration.[93] However, a clean transition in practice is muddled by Note 17 in the Notes following the texts in the main Common Worship Book: there, under 'The Taking', the Note includes: 'The bread and wine must be taken into the president's hands and replaced upon the table either after the table has been prepared *or during the Eucharistic Prayer*' (editorial emphasis added). So, although within the rite the heading 'Taking of the

---

[92] The sub-group included Bryan Spinks, who had published work on the East Syrian anaphora of Addai and Mari, which has no narrative.

[93] See the discussion under 'epiclesis' on pp.103-106 below.

Bread and Wine' has the instruction *'The president takes the bread and wine'*, this Note 17 permits the president to ignore the instruction and embark on a thanksgiving, and then do the taking during the narrative, i.e. *in via*. This blurs the clean lines of the fourfold shape which had been achieved with much labour. Any implications for consecration can only be subjectively determined.

(f) Anamnesis

'Anamnesis' is simple transliteration into English of the Greek ἀναμνησις, and the paragraph after the narrative has been universally called the 'anamnesis'. Its origins appear to have been, as its grammar dictates, a declaration of how the people celebrating the sacrament fulfil the Lord's command, the verbal climax of the narrative: 'Do this in remembrance of me', and the anamnesis responds 'Therefore we...' Ancient texts of the anamnesis vary considerably, though Hippolytus has a simply worded form, 'Remembering therefore his death and resurrection, we offer to you the bread and cup...' In both East and West more complex forms developed, and the Sarum text (*Unde et memores*) ran:

> Therefore also, Lord, we your servants, but also your holy people, having in remembrance the blessed passion of our Son Christ our Lord, likewise his resurrection from the dead, and also his glorious ascension into heaven, do offer to your excellent majesty from your gifts and bounty a pure victim, a holy victim, an unblemished victim, the holy bread of eternal life and the cup of everlasting salvation.

The Reformers provided in English in **1549** an even more complex sentence than this. But crucially they replaced its main verb 'we...do offer [the victim]' with 'we do celebrate and make here before thy divine majesty...the memorial which thy Son hath willed us to make.' If Sarum was offering a 'victim' (and presumably Christ, the sacrificial victim?) to the Father, **1549** was now cautiously saying that, whatever Jesus had 'willed' the sacrament to be, whatever 'memorial' meant, that was what the church was now doing. In **1552** Cranmer, believing that the Lord's command was that we should eat the bread and drink the wine, dispensed with an anamnesis verbalizing our response to his command, and instead ordered the actual eating and drinking to be that response. Thus **1662, RtA/80** BCP- Order, and **CW/00**(OrdTwo) all display exactly this shape, the communion being the response to 'Do this'.

Scottish **1637** reverted to the **1549** shape and thus restored the anamnesis, with its main verb repeating from **1549** 'we... with these thy holy gifts', make the memorial which thy Son hath willed us to make...'. The Scottish **1764**, which became definitive, largely followed **1637**, continuing a model of the 'long prayer'.

Many in the Church of England, from the mid-19th century onwards, have also wanted a 'long prayer' of consecration. Some have moved the 'Prayer of oblation' to follow the narrative; others have slipped in the Roman canon (sometimes said silently after the **1662** consecration); and some have sighed for **1549**.[94]   Walter Frere, citing the example of both **1549** and Scottish **1637**, proposed in 1911 'a simple and small step' – the 'reannexation' of the Prayer of Oblation to the Prayer of Consecration. He made no proposal for an anamnesis, suggesting a mere 'Wherefore' to connect the prayer of oblation to the dominical command.[95]   However, the theological Conference which was called to compose a text in 1919-20 declined to locate the self-oblation within the lengthened prayer, but it did expand the linking words into a verbal anamnesis. Thereafter the run-up to 1927 and **1928** led to an expanded final text:

---

[94] The various strands are charted in Mark Dalby, *Anglican Missals and their Canons: 1549, Interim Rite and Roman* (Alcuin/GROW Joint Liturgical Study 41, Grove Books, Cambridge, 1998).

[95] W.H.Frere, *Some Principles of Liturgical Reform* (John Murray, London, 1911) p.191-194. Dalby labels this minimal addition, leading into the 'prayer of oblation', as 'Overall's canon', following what was attributed to Bishop Overall in the seventeenth century.

> Wherefore, O Lord and heavenly Father, we thy humble servants, having in remembrance the death and passion of thy dear Son, his mighty resurrection and glorious ascension, according to his holy institution, do celebrate and set forth before thy Divine Majesty with these thy holy gifts the memorial which he hath willed us to make, rendering unto thee most hearty thanks for the innumerable benefits which he hath procured unto us.

This also restored the self-oblation to the latter part of the prayer. In the event the **1928** Prayer of Consecration attracted little following, as few wanted the 'Eastern' position of the epiclesis. Dalby's account of anglo-catholic unofficial initiatives in the years following indicates that, along with both exotic Roman uses and some nostalgia for **1549**, the minimal provision of 'Overall's Canon' held a strong place as the 'IntrmRt' (and could be read almost directly from **1662**'s printed page). However, the *Altar Missal* in 1936 included as one option, in Dalby's words, 'the canon of the interim rite, "now widely used and sanctioned" and now printed with an anamnesis, albeit a silent one.'[96] A revised edition followed in 1939, still containing the 'Interim Rite', and 'a public anamnesis was added for the first time'. [97] Thus when the bishops came to edit existing uses in 1965 to provide S1/65 among proposed texts, their anamnesis read:

> Wherefore, O Lord and heavenly Father, we thy humble servants, having in remembrance the precious death and passion of thy dear Son, his mighty resurrection and glorious ascension, entirely desire thy fatherly goodness mercifully to accept this our sacrifice of praise and thanksgiving…

---

[96] Dalby, *op.cit.*, p.30
[97] *Id.*, p.31

This text was authorized within **S1/66**, and recurred within **S1-2/76(A)** and **RtB/80(1)**. However, the contemporary speech form which became RtA/80(4) saw a shift of emphasis:

Therefore, Lord and heavenly Father,
in remembrance of the precious death and passion,
the mighty resurrection and glorious ascension
of your dear Son Jesus Christ.
we offer you through him this sacrifice of praise and thanksgiving…

The differences continued in 1998-200. **CW/00(OrdOneTrad(C))** repeated the 'traditional' text from the earlier versions; and OrdOne(C) repeated the Prayer from **RtA/80** (though with 'our' inserted between 'this' and 'sacrifice'). Curiously, the central action of **1549**, of the Scottish developments, and of **1928**, namely, 'we make the memorial', did not reappear, perhaps because the anamnesis in IntrmRt had been rebuilt from the bare 'wherefore' of Frere's original proposal.

The original Hippolytus text, which was Couratin's model in 1964-66, ran:

Remembering therefore his death and resurrection, we offer to you the bread and cup, giving thanks to you…

Couratin delivered Hippolytus' text almost *verbatim* as the main statement of how the church is acting in obedience to Jesus' command. This proved controversial and was amended in 1966-67.[98] The text replacing 'we offer' revived **1549** – 'with this bread and this cup we make the memorial of his saving passion, etc.' But the Liturgical Commission, seeing 'make the memorial' as an unsatisfactory stopgap, soon replaced

---

[98] See the account on p.16 and pp.63-65 above.

it with 'celebrate [the mighty acts of God]' in **S3/73** and then resisted attempts to restore 'make the memorial' for **RtA/80**. 'Make the memorial' ran on in texts derived from **S2/67**, such as **S1-2/76(2)**, **RtA/80(2)** and **RtB/80(2)**. This history was ignored when it was preferred to 'we celebrate' at the assimilation of the first two prayers of **RtA/80** into the single Eucharistic Prayer A in **CW/00**(OrdOne). The prayer which then became **RtA/80(3)** and **CW/00**(OrdOne(C)) also featured 'memorial', though in the form 'we celebrate this memorial...'[99] This was in curious contrast to the IntrmRt, **S1/66**, and their descendants, which had 'make the memorial' in their genes, but did not retain it in the post-1928 generations.

While the two sets of anamneses examined above developed by discernible stages, the same cannot well be said of the other prayers – the ones with no ancestry – in CW. There is certainly no commonality to their anamneses, though overall they cover broadly the same areas of Christian truth.

CW/00(D)	CW/00(F)	CW/00(G)	CW/00(H)	Additional Euch Prayer One	Additional Euch Prayer Two
Therefore, Father, with this bread and this cup we celebrate the cross on which he died to make us free. Defying death he rose again and is alive with you to plead for us and all the world.	So, Father, we remember all that Jesus did, In him we plead with confidence his sacrifice made once for all upon the cross. Bringing before you the bread of life and cup of salvation, we proclaim his death and resurrection until he comes in glory.	Therefore we proclaim the death that he suffered on the cross, we celebrate his resurrection, his bursting from the tomb, we rejoice that he reigns at your right hand on high and we long for his coming in glory. As we recall the one perfect sacrifice of our redemption [lead into the epiclesis]	[after each half of narrative] **Father, we do this in remembrance of him; his body is the bread of life** *and* **his blood is shed for all.** As we proclaim his death and celebrate his rising in glory, [lead into the epiclesis]	Father, as we bring this bread and wine, and remember his death and resurrection [lead into the epiclesis]	So Father with this bread and cup we celebrate his love, his death, his risen life. [lead into the 'second epiclesis']

Clearly, any sense that an anamnesis must have a single given set of

---

[99] . See the texts as they developed from 1978 on pp.66-67 above.

words or sequence of thought had gone, though possibly an awareness of what should *not* be said had set some limits on the freedom of drafting. The actual texts tend to phase into the epiclesis which follows, as, e.g., in Prayer F the exposition of Christ's death as his sacrifice comes at the beginning of the epiclesis, and in both F and G (see page 76 above for its text) the bread and wine have no mention in the anamnesis, but are explicitly named in the epiclesis following.

The wording of the anamnesis had been the storm-centre in 1966-67, but, once the controversial explicit offering of the elements to God had been excised, the church found various ways to say that, in obedience to Jesus' command, it keeps his remembrance, notably of his sacrificial death and resurrection. Across the whole range of eight prayers in 1998-2000, very little of the text of the different anamneses was referred back to the Revision Committee.

(g) Epiclesis[100]

Epiclesis is simply a transliteration of the Greek ἐπικλησις, literally calling on or down, appealing, invocation: the movement is in the opposite direction to offering. The primitive direct 'Come, Holy Spirit' gradually changed into a petition asking God the Father to send the Holy Spirit to consecrate or 'eucharistize' the bread and wine. Where this petition is placed is bound up with, if not determined by, the church's view of consecration. Both before and after the Reformation the Church of England's texts had followed the Latin, Western, pattern where, because the narrative had in Roman dogma a strongly consecratory role, a precatory pre-narrative epiclesis naturally led into it. So **1549**, which still located consecration in the narrative, kept the prayer in the same place, but added reference to the Spirit: 'Hear us (o merciful Father) we beseech thee; and with thy Holy Spirit and word, vouchsafe to bless and sanctify

---

[100] A close study of the epiclesis in the Church of England from 1945 to 2000 is in David J. Kennedy, *Eucharistic Sacramentality in an Ecumenical Context: The Anglican Epiclesis* (Ashgate, Aldershot, 2008) pp.139-169.

these thy gifts, and creatures of bread and wine...' In 1552 Cranmer kept the prayer in this 'Western' position, but altered its thrust to ask for God's empowering of the giving and receiving of the bread and wine: 'Grant that we, receiving these thy creatures...may be partakers of his most blessed body and blood'.[101] This is the text that has persisted through **1559** and **1662** to this day, though **1662** itself and its descendants have restored a concept of consecration through the dominical words in the narrative. The pre-narrative petition, in its **1549** form '...that they may be unto us', was similarly employed in the new drafting which began with S2/65.[102] This continued to **RtA/80**, with an insertion of 'by the power of your Spirit' being added to S3/71 during revision, so that from **S3/73** onwards the petition has had this explicit mention of 'your Spirit', which in **RtA/80** became 'your Holy Spirit'. From **S1-2/76** onwards the same addition has been made to the **1662** 'receptionist' form of the petition, though it does not occur in the strictly **1662** forms in the appendix to **RtA/80** and in **CW/00**(OrdTwo). So **RtA/80**(4) had 'grant that by the power of your Holy Spirit we who receive these gifts of your creation, this bread and this wine, according to your Son our Saviour Jesus Christ's holy institution, in remembrance of the death that he suffered, may be partakers...'.

The change to an 'Eastern' position was well placarded by the 1986-91 Liturgical Commission in their 1989 *Patterns*.[103] In their four eucharistic prayers, an epiclesis invoking the Spirit came in a variety of forms, but in each case in this 'Eastern' position. The change was well explained and reinforced when Tom Talley,[104] speaking at the 1993 meeting of the

---

[101] See Colin Buchanan, *What did Cranmer Think He was Doing?* (Grove Liturgical 7, Grove Books, Bramcote, 1976) p.22.

[102] As shown earlier, Couratin, like Dix, was fundamentally Western in his doctrinal understanding..

[103] See their outline of the prayer's structure on p.56 above.

[104] Then Professor Emeritus of Liturgy at the General Theological Seminary, New York. See David R. Holeton, *Revising the Eucharist* (Alcuin/GROW Joint Liturgical Study 27, Bramcote, 1994).

IALC, showed that the epiclesis occurs where the church's praise turns to prayer. This pattern of the Eastern church, where the Christological praise, preceded by praise to the Creator ending in the Sanctus, reaches its climax in the narrative, followed by a mix of anamnesis and epiclesis leading into petition, had been abandoned by the Roman, Western, church in the fourth century.

While the location of the epiclesis remains a major issue, a question also relates to its form. The difference between **1549** and **1552** is noted above, and the **1549** form 'that they may be to us' was proposed by the Commission in S2/65 as providing a broadly inclusive petition for consecration without specifying how consecration was viewed as occurring. However, the relocation of the epiclesis in *Patterns* came from a Commission interested in pushing out the boundaries in innovative rites, and ready for very varied forms. The petition in Prayers B and C that the Spirit would 'show' the elements to be the body and blood of Christ raised its own problems in Synod.[105]   In Prayer A the petition was that the Spirit would 'flow through us', and in Prayer D it was 'Pour out your Holy Spirit as we bring before you these gifts'; and both cases seem distant from any very specific doctrine of consecration. However Prayer B was far more specific in its 'Pour out your Holy Spirit over us and these gifts'. While various Eastern texts do call for the Spirit to descend on the elements, the previous texts in the Church of England had been far less precise, and, in the beliefs of many, the Spirit's work was to be sought in the eucharistic action, not in entering into the actual elements. And, as this Prayer B became what we have called above 'the great survivor', the text of its epiclesis roused concerns. So it was that, when Trevor Lloyd introduced it to Synod in November 1994, Colin Buchanan from the floor remarked 'The line "Pour out your Holy Spirit over us and these your gifts" always reminds me of custard.' This carried the Synod and the text was altered in the Revision Committee. When the Prayer was

---

[105] See p.30 above.

resuscitated as **CW/00**(OrdOne(G)), for some reason the calling of the Spirit onto the elements was restored, and had again to be removed. But the general quest for variety continued and the epiclesis in the Eastern position in Prayers D,F.G and H and in Prayer One of the 2012 Additional Prayers has no one grammatical structure or theological weighting at all.

(h) Petition for Fruitful Reception and Doxology

The eucharistic prayer, in this final section of petition, usually asks that the receiving of communion may be fruitful in the recipients. In Western-type prayers (as identified above) this takes the form of a 'second epiclesis'. In the IntrmRt and **S1/66** line of descendants from **1662** the petition has come in the parts of the so-called 'Prayer of oblation' which returned from the post-communion to fulfil this role. The key words which express its role pray 'that all we, who are partakers of this holy communion, may be fulfilled with thy grace and heavenly benediction'. This is found in all 'traditional' texts from S1/65 through to **CW/00**(OrdOneTrad), and also in 'contemporary' language in **RtA/80**(4) and **CW/00**(OrdOne(C)).

The Hippolytan texts took shape by stages. In S2/65, the draft said simply 'we pray thee to accept this our service and service in the presence of thy divine majesty', without visible mention of reception. In S2/66 Couratin had redrafted it as: 'we pray thee to accept this our duty and service and grant that we may so eat these holy things in the presence of thy divine majesty, that we may be filled with thy grace and heavenly blessing'. Thus it was authorized in **S2/67**, but the language change to S3/71 ushered in the transitive verbs in the active: 'As we eat and drink these holy gifts in the presence of your divine majesty, renew us by your Spirit; inspire us with your love; and unite us in the body of your Son...' So the text has continued through **RtA/80**(1) and into **CW/00**(OrdOne and OrdOneTrad).[106] **RtA/80**(2), though based in **S2/67**, collected the

---

[106] There was a brief hiccup, described on p.66 and note 42 above where this wording might have been lost.

new drafting about the 'holy temple', and when this Prayer was assimilated into **CW/00**(A), the 'holy temple' moved across to **CW/00**(G).[107]

The Brindley-Beckwith text which became **RtA/80**(3) and **CW/00**(B), began with an oddity in that Hippolytus had an Eastern epiclesis, but Rome, in Eucharistic Prayer II, had inserted a Western-type epiclesis before the narrative, and, as might be expected, had omitted Hippolytus' epiclesis. Brindley for some reason had both – the Western 'first epiclesis' was there, and then after the anamnesis Brindley turned Hippolytus' text 'Send your Holy Spirit upon the offering of your holy Church' into 'Send your Holy Spirit upon all that your church sets before you'. The Revision Committee in 1978-79 changed this to 'Send your Holy Spirit upon your people and gather into one in your kingdom all who share...', and this nicely became a prayer for fruitful reception, and continued so through to **CW/00**(B),

After this, new prayers expressed this petition in different ways. RtC/89 displayed great variety, including, in Prayer B, insertions at this point, each actually asking for fruitful reception in different ways, as the matrix did not specify the benefits of reception at all.[108] The RtC/89 Prayers more or less reappeared in the **95-96** texts, but were then defeated in Synod.

The further new Prayers in **CW** emphasized in the epiclesis the coming of the Spirit on the people to make their participation fruitful, rather as in **RtA/80**(3) quoted above. In D, E,F and G there is a strong eschatological dimension, with feasting in the heavenly kingdom as the ultimate 'fruit' of communion; and F and G provide brief space for intercessions. The 2012 Additional Prayers also ask for the Spirit to come upon the communicants and to bring them to the eternal glory.

Apart from the strict **1662** texts, the eucharistic prayer normally ends with a doxology and a congregational affirmation in an (acclamatory)

---

[107] See the text in the table on p.76 above.
[108] See the text in the table on p.76 above. The provision continued in **95-96**(2), but was changed in **CW/00**(OrdOne)(G).

'Amen'. In S3/71 the Commission built up the response with 'Blessing and honour and glory and power...' drawn from Rev.7.12. This was sustained in **RtA/80**(1), but did not appear then in others. In *Patterns* RtC/89 used it in Prayers A and C (Prayers B and D both ended with the Sanctus) and in **95-96** Prayers 2, 4 and 6 ended with it, while Prayers 1, 3 and 5 with different texts from Revelation provided a new range of two-line congregational acclamatory doxologies. In **CW/00**(OrdOne) Prayers A, D and G have the Rev.7.12 text, while Prayer H concludes with the Sanctus. The other four stay with 'Amen'. The 2012 Additional Prayers both conclude with 'Amen', though the characteristic feature of Prayer One is preserved in showing 'Amen, Amen, Amen' for three different groups of voices.

(i) Supplementary Consecration

In **1662** very precise rubrical instructions provided both for the consecration of the elements during the reading of the narrative, and for supplementary consecration of additional bread or wine by a repetition of the relevant dominical words from the narrative. **1928** made no provision in the Alternative Order, but must have presumed that **1662** arrangements would continue; and the same would seem to apply to **S1/66**. However, in **S1-2/76** specific provision was made, following the pattern adopted slightly earlier for **S3/73**, as shown below. **RtB/80** and **CW/00**(OrdOneTrad) conformed to the same pattern.

The new rites followed an odd route. In the initial S2/65 a final rubric ordered both bread and wine to be placed on the table, and the president was then to '*read the Prayer of Consecration, beginning at* "Hear us, O Father", *and ending at* "through the same Christ our Lord" [ie after the anamnesis]'. The Commission itself viewed this as over-elaborate, and deleted it. In the Introduction to S2/66 they reported the omission and 'suggested' that *pro tem* **1662** use should be followed – in effect, acknowledging that the **1662** rubric had no legal standing in a new service; and thus **S2/67** was authorized with no provision made. A wide discussion elicited a principle that, once the great Thanksgiving had been uttered, further bread and wine could be brought into the context thus created and that would consecrate them 'by extension'. The Doctrine Commission was approached, and their confidential memorandum supported 'extending the context', and recommended taking further supplies in silence. For S3/71 the Commission accepted silence but also, as an alternative, drafted a spoken text :

> Having given thanks to you, Father, over the bread and cup, as your Son our Lord Jesus Christ commanded, we receive this bread/wine also as his body/blood.

A Synod member in February 1972 appealed to Michael Ramsey for his judgment of taking more in silence. He replied:

> After all, the consecration…is one of most stupendous things that ever happens in the physical world… What I shudder from with my whole being is the thought of this reconsecration, by being silent, taking place without the Christian community in the building knowing it is happening.[109]

The option of silence was duly excised, and the Steering Committee inserted an actual quotation of Jesus' words into the spoken formula, and thus in **S3/73** it took the form it still retains, and that wording has recurred in both traditional and contemporary texts at each new drafting of rites since 1973.

(j) The Lord's Prayer
The text of the Lord's Prayer is discussed in the Appendix below. Its

---

[109] *See Report of Proceedings of General Synod* (February 1972). Note that (a) Michael Ramsey used the inherited (misleading) term, 'reconsecration', and (b) he was not questioning that the proposal truly 'consecrated' the elements. Silence recurs in the Church of Ireland 2004 BCP.

location in eucharistic liturgy fits here after treatment of the eucharistic prayer itself. In **1662** it began the rite and then began the post-communion. In **CW/00** this continues in OrdTwo but is changed in OrdTwoContmp to allow the opening use to be optional. **1928**, IntrmRt and **S1/66** all adopted the Roman pattern where the Lord's Prayer follows immediately upon the eucharistic prayer. However, in introducing **S2/65** Jasper invoked 'its older position, after the Fraction, as the immediate prelude to the act of Communion. The petitions...make it peculiarly suitable at this point.'[110]   This position was sustained in **S2/67** and also in **S3/73**, but the weight of synodical opinion in 1978-79 favoured current Rome over 'its older position', and the Lord's Prayer was duly linked to the eucharistic prayer in all the rites except the strictly **1662** ones.

12. The Breaking of the Bread

The breaking of the bread, once accepted by the Commission as the third feature of the fourfold 'shape', was presented thereafter as a discrete item within the rite. Cranmer had given it little prominence. The '*somewhat larger*' **1549** wafers were to be broken in two during distribution; and in **1552** without rubrical direction the bread, which was '*the best and purest wheat bread...*', must have been broken during the distribution. Thus the Puritans at the Savoy Conference in 1661, when complaining that the consecration was not explicit, added that 'breaking of the bread is not so much as mentioned.'[111]   The revisers then ordered by indented rubrics five manual acts during the narrative. So now the officiant was not only to lay a hand upon the elements to consecrate them with the dominical words, but also to accompany 'he brake it' with an actual breaking of the bread. As the narrative continued on, there was no wholesale breaking of the '*best and purest Wheat Bread*'. So for practical distribution it had to be broken in some relatively unnoticed way. As breaking bread

---

[110] Liturgical Commission, *Alternative Services: Second Series* (SPCK, 1965) p.148.
[111] See Colin Buchanan, *The Savoy Conference Revisited* (Alcuin/GROW Joint Liturgical Study 54, Grove Books, Cambridge, 2002), Exception 31 p.48.

during the narrative did not serve the distribution, it must have been thought in some way symbolic, or simply a demonstration of following faithfully Jesus' Last Supper.[112] Locating the fraction within the narrative is almost unique in liturgical history. The rubrics and manual acts continued through the IntrmRt and into S1/65 and **S1/66**. However, Dix's 'fourfold' shape then began to impact revision, and so in these rites the indented rubric read '*And here he may break the bread*'. This '*may*' allowed provision after the eucharistic prayer: '*Here the Priest is to break the Bread, if it be not already broken*'. These alternative locations ran on through the first Thanksgiving in **S1-2/76** and in **RtB/80**. However, in **CW/00**(OrdOneTrad) the text conformed to the order of OrdOne; all indented rubrics disappeared from the eucharistic prayers, and the breaking of the bread was always to follow the Lord's Prayer. However, **RtA/80** BCP-Order, and both forms of **CW/00**(OrdTwo), retained **1662**'s original indented rubrics, with the breaking of the bread as the second manual act.

Dix came slowly into these **1662** descendants, yet, because his fourfold shape, including the breaking of the bread, was a given in all the Commission's new drafting, the separated item came swiftly in new rites; the only issue was about spoken text to accompany it. The Commission set aside any supposed dramatization of Calvary, but instead saw the breaking as articulating mutual sharing; so Paul's words in 1 Corinthians 10.16-17 could hardly have been more apt. Thus in S2/65, S2/66 and **S2/67** these two verses were set out in lines, initially to be a triad of versicles and responses, but finally for (optional) corporate recitation throughout.

---

[112] It seems likely that the Puritans after the consecration viewed the breaking of bread and pouring of wine as being used 'to represent and commemorate the sacrifice of Christ's body and blood' (see, e.g., E.C.Ratcliff, 'Puritan Alternatives to the Prayer Book' in *The English Prayer Book 1549-1662* (Alcuin/SPCK, 1963) p.77). Behind this lay probably the King James Version of 1 Cor.11.24; and 'broken for you' appears in Hippolytus's narrative, and in various later texts, but without overt links to the physical breaking of the bread. 'Broken for you' did not appear in Sarum, nor in Cranmer's liturgies, but the Puritans almost certainly worked more directly from the KJV.

In 1970-71 the Commission decided against St Paul's order of starting with the cup for a section solely about the bread, and for S3/71 and thereafter they drafted a single (but now mandatory) versicle and response:

We break this bread
to share in the body of Christ.
Though we are many, we are one body,
because we all share in the one bread.

The traditional-language **S1-2/76** and **RtB/80** gained the same versicle and response, though still under the rubric '*The priest breaks the consecrated bread, if he has not already done so, saying...*'. In each rite, the second eucharistic prayer (from **S2/67**), has no option of breaking the bread within the narrative, and so the breaking would occur here, with the mandatory versicle and response.

Patterns for Worship (1989) widened the field. A section entitled 'Words at the Breaking of the Bread', tucked within the chapter 'Introductory Words', offered texts for seven different seasons or occasions, mostly in a responsive form.[113]   Further forms followed as printed after the Lord's Prayer at the end of Eucharistic Prayers A, C and D. In B and D the existing 1 Cor.10.16-17 text was provided, but Prayer A had a longer text to match the 'Taking' text at the beginning of the prayer:

We are one with Christ in praise and glory,
heirs together of his kingdom.
We break this bread to share in his body.
We take and eat to proclaim his death today.
We live by faith in the promises of his covenant.
We have this wine to share in his blood.

---

[113] See Liturgical Commission, *Patterns for Worship* (CIO, 1989) pp.237-238.

We take and drink to proclaim his death today.

A new volume of *Patterns* was published by CHP in 1995 in hardback format and now commended for actual liturgical use. Because the Bishops had not introduced RtC/89 into Synod, this comprehensive volume was in theory commending simply non-eucharistic material. Nevertheless eleven of the 17 'Sample Services' were eucharistic. Ten of them provided 'We break this bread...' to accompany the breaking; but one had from 1 Cor.11.26 'Every time we eat this bread and drink this cup, we proclaim....'. This came in Lent and Holy Week in the 1989 proposals. One further sample service made it alternative to the standard form; and in a further one again the 1989 text for 'creation' etc now recurred to accompany the standard text.

Curiously, **CW/00** itself, despite its general multiplication of seasonal materials, provided simply the two alternatives – 'We break this bread to share...' or 'As often as we eat this bread...'[114] *Times and Seasons* (2006) went back to proposals in the original 1989 *Patterns* and commended the Epiphany text there for four seasonal occasions and, with a little tweaking, adapted three others for three further seasonal occasions.

13. Invitation and distribution

In **1552** Cranmer moved the distribution close to the narrative, as the distribution was becoming the immediate obedience to Jesus' command 'Do this'. He commanded; so we do it; and the president does not need an additional verbal invitation.[115] The **1552** words of distribution ('Take

---

[114] Though the Commission had in front of it the 1979 ECUSA *Book of Occasional Offices* where there are 15 'confractoria' there is hardly any overlap between the two. The *Patterns* list was expanded to 12 in the 1994 Bishops' report *Eucharistic Prayers* (GS1120), section VIII 'Alternative Words at the Breaking of Bread'.

[115] That had arguably come earlier, in the introduction to the penitential section 'Draw near and receive this holy sacrament to your comfort' (which **1662** had reinforced, from Heb.10.22, into 'Draw near with faith and...'), but that implied no physical movement, for it was to be done 'meekly kneeling upon your knees'

and eat this in remembrance...' and 'Drink this in remembrance...') provided explanation; though the combination in **1559** of the two sets of words of distribution from **1549** and **1552** provided weightier texts somewhat lengthier to deliver. Then, once the Laudians had made placed communion tables solidly against East walls, communicants physically approached a rail or step. Still no spoken text invited them, but communicants generally came forward when the distribution was clearly going to begin. When **1928** and IntrmRt separated the distribution from the narrative, there was more need for an invitation. So now the weight of the words of distribution could be moved into a single invitation, to be addressed to all the communicants corporately, rather than said to each one individually. Thus **S1/66** retained the **1662** words of distribution, but, as an option, the words for bread and cup could be combined into a single invitation:

> Draw near with faith: Receive the body of our Lord Jesus Christ, which was given for you, and his blood, which was shed for you. Take this in remembrance that Christ died for you, and feed on him in your hearts by faith with thanksgiving.

S1/66 then allowed the words spoken to each communicant to be simply half of **1662**'s respective formulae, for both bread and cup. The Commission was somewhat more radical - in S2/65: the invitation was there (shorn of 'Take this in remembrance that Christ died for you'), but the only words of distribution were the minimal 'The Body of Christ' and 'The Blood of Christ' with the response 'Amen'. Then in S2/66 the invitation itself disappeared, but the **1662** words of distribution were restored as an option instead of 'The Body/Blood of Christ'. The Convocations then restored the invitation as an option; but it remained possible in **S2/67** to use no verbal invitation and only the short words said in distribution.

In S3/71 the Commission stepped back slightly from **S2/67**'s permission for such stark wording. The invitation was amended and made mandatory, and the words of distribution expanded to 'The Body/ Blood of Christ keep you in eternal life'. This was benedictional, sustaining **1662**'s grammar, but shortening the text enough for the communicant to say 'Amen' before receiving. This text was authorized as **S3/73**.

While this modern text was looking disciplined, the revisions in the **1662** line were allowing alternatives. **S1-2/76** introduced a new variant on 'Draw near'. It remained 'Draw near with faith' in the invitation, but also came earlier as an alternative call to repentance, set in parallel with **1662**'s 'Draw near with faith, and take this holy sacrament...'

> Seeing we have a great high priest who has passed into the heavens, Jesus the Son of God, let us draw near with a true heart in full assurance of faith, and make our confession to our heavenly Father.[116]

This certainly gave a clear understanding to 'draw near', and it continued in 1980 in **RtB/80** but never penetrated into **RtA/80** or subsequent rites.

In the years 1978-80, the existing uses from **S3/73** and **S1-2/76** were continued in the main texts in both **RtA/80** and **RtB/80**. However, an appendix to **RtA/80** provided other possibilities, signalled by cross-references in the rite. These new texts for the invitation were 'additional' to the main text: one Roman Catholic one, one Eastern, and one drawn from the Roman Catholic provision for the acclamation of the Gospel on Easter Day.

---

[116] This text (following John Cosin in 1661) thus took the major part of Heb.10.22 into the liturgy.

| Jesus is the Lamb of God
who takes away the sins of the world.
Happy are those who are called to his supper.
Lord, I am not worthy to receive you,
but only say the word, and I shall be healed.[117] | The gifts of God for the people of God.
Jesus Christ is holy,
Jesus Christ is Lord,
to the glory of God the Father.

(Easter Day to Pentecost)
Alleluia! Christ our Passover is sacrificed for us.
Alleluia! Let us keep the feast. |

The different words for distribution were 'alternatives' - *viz* full **1662** words.

CW/00(OrdOneTrad) moved the confession to the beginning of the rite and introduced it in the same terms as in OrdOne. Thus the call, 'Draw near with a true heart...', disappeared. In OrdOne, in both forms, 'Draw near with faith' remained in the invitation to communion, but the alternatives from the appendix in **RtA/80** (shown above) were all now within the main text, and in OrdOneTrad they had been adapted back into Tudor language. In OrdTwo, as in **1662** itself, there could be no verbal invitation after the narrative; but the call to confession retained the traditional 'Draw near with faith'.

14. Post-communion prayers and Dismissal

1662 had a post-communion section which remained untouched within the **RtA/80** BCP-Order and in both forms of OrdTwo in 2000. However, it was whittled away as the IntrmRt and **S1/66** adopted an overall shape somewhat like the Roman mass, and this shaped the new services also. The two tables here on page 118 enable the trends to be seen.

The two prayers printed in **CW/00** (OrdOne) have interesting origins. In the 1960s the Liturgical Commission abandoned the Frere-**1928**-IntrmRt inclusion of self-oblation within the Prayer of Consecration, and returned to the **1552/1662** use of it as responsive to God's grace received in communion. An adapted **1662** prayer came in S2/65, and

---

[117] The proposal for the first line to the Revision Committee by Brian Brindley was the full Roman 'Behold the Lamb of God' ('Ecce, Agnus Dei'), but the Committee accepted it in this form.

could be said corporately; but in March 1966 a small group of the Commission produced a succinct streamlined form which has remained unchanged (though gaining contemporary language) ever since. Cyril Bowles played a key part in this. From S3/71 onwards it has been printed for congregational recitation.

The second prayer is David Frost's 'Father of all', written by him in contemporary form for S3/71 for presidential use, replacing the run-on in **S2/67** of the **1662** Prayer of Thanksgiving. Because it was in the post-communion, Synod did not get far enough on the first day of the initial Revision Stage in November 1971 to dismiss it summarily, as it had dismissed the two earlier Frost prayers.[118]   When the revision was resumed in February 1972, wiser counsels prevailed and the post-communion prayer was spared. It continued as a presidential monologue in **RtA/80**, but was printed for congregational recitation in **CW/00**.[119]

The ending of the service had in S2/65 a notable omission – there was no blessing. A theory existed that receiving communion was the greatest liturgical blessing and adding a verbal blessing to it was otiose and misleading. There was simply a brief dismissal. The Convocations never bought the theory, and a blessing, though still optional, was added before authorization as **S2/67**. The idea has almost certainly died, and although the rubrics in subsequent rites can just be understood as permission to

---

[118] As mentioned on p.20 and note 26 above, this was known on the Commission as the night of the long knives

[119] There was fiddling with what is nowadays line 10. Frost had written 'Anchor us in this hope that we have grasped' (see S3/71), and the Revision Committee changed this to 'Keep us in this hope that have grasped' (see **S3/73**). This was proposed by the Commission in RtA/78, but was changed by the Revision Committee to 'Keep us firm in the hope you have set before us' (see RtA/79), which has continued since. It is uncertain whether David Frost approved the changes.

Table of post-communion in rites following 1662

1662 (in 1662 order)	S1/66	S1-2/76	RtB/80	CW/00 (OrdOneTrad)
		Optional proper sentence	Optional proper sentence	Post-communion prayer
Lord's Prayer	Alternative after the Prayer of Consecration or here (text printed in both places)	Alternative after the Thanksgiving, or after the Breaking of the Bread, or here (text in latter two places)	Alternative after the Thanksgiving, or after the Breaking of the Bread, or here (text only in second place)	Only ordered (and printed) after Eucharistic Prayer
(*Alternatives*) 'Prayer of Oblation'	In two alternative ways part of the Prayer of Consecration, but also printed for use in whole or in part here.	Part within the Thanksgiving. Succinct form from **S2/67** printed here second. Full text in Appendix.	Part within the Thanksgiving. Succinct form from **S2/67** printed here. Full text in Appendix.	Part within the Thanksgiving. Succinct form from **S2/67** here. Or '*another suitable prayer.*'
(*or*) 'Prayer of thanksgiving'	Between two forms of 'prayer of oblation' *or* Prayer of self-offering (drawn from 1662)	Printed as first prayer before succinct form from **S2/67**	Printed as first prayer before succinct form from **S2/67**	Printed as first prayer before succinct form from **S2/67**. Or from '*those in the Appendix*'
Gloria in Excelsis	Rubric allows it at beginning of rite. Text printed at end only.	Text printed at beginning of rite. Rubric allows it at end.	Text printed at beginning of rite. Rubric allows it at end.	Text printed at beginning of rite only. No mention at end.
Blessing	Blessing as 1662	Blessing as 1662; dismissal added	Blessing as 1662; dismissal added	Blessing as 1662; dismissal added

Table of post-communion in new rites

S2/67	S3/73	RtA/80	CW/00(OrdOne)
	Optional high seasonal sentence	Optional sentence of each Sunday and optional hymn	Post-communion prayer of each Sunday ('*or another suitable prayer*')
Prayer of thanksgiving (slightly adapted from 1662) *or* Prayer of self-offering (drawn from 1662)	New prayer 'Father of all' drafted by David Frost *or* Prayer of self-offering (drawn from 1662)	'Father of all' by David Frost *or* Prayer of self-offering (as **S3/73**)	'Father of all' by David Frost *or* Prayer of self-offering (as **S3/73**)
Optional Gloria in Excelsis	Optional hymn or canticle		
Dismissal *or/and* Blessing (as 1662)	Blessing (including seasonal blessing) Dismissal	Blessing (including seasonal blessing) Dismissal	Blessing (including seasonal blessing) Dismissal

omit a blessing, the presentation (and general usage) keep the blessing as normal. The dismissal goes back to the S2/65 proposal, and since S3/71 it has followed the blessing.

15. Consumption of remains

In **1552** no consecrated elements remained at the end of the eucharist; without any objective consecration, a closing rubric laconically allowed '*And if any of the bread or wine remain, the Curate shall have it to his own use.*' However, **1662** imposed a very clear concept of an objective consecration upon Cranmer's text, and included a direction as to how the remains should be treated. The second rubric after the distribution now read:

When all have communicated, the Minister shall return to the Lord's Table, and reverently place upon it what remains of the consecrated Elements, covering the same with a fair linen cloth.

Then the sixth rubric at the end of the service was drafted accordingly:

...if any remain of that which was consecrated, it shall not be carried out of the Church, but the Priest and such other of the Communicants as he shall then call unto him, shall immediately after the Blessing, reverently eat and drink the same.[120]

So here was a clear pattern of consumption. It was not to happen within the rite, but to come immediately after its conclusion – and be done on the premises.[121] It was this latter rubric which was at stake when 19th century controversies about reservation of consecrated elements arose. In broad terms, the elements remained covered on the communion table, though the coming of credence tables also invited the return of the remains to that side-table. At the same time there came a new term from

---

[120] The extraordinary document of ARCIC-2, *Clarifications* (SPCK/CTS, 1994), expounds 'reverently' in this rubric as indicating that 1662 expected, or at least allowed, Anglicans to adore Christ present in the consecrated elements. See Colin Buchanan, *Did the Anglicans and Roman Catholics agree on the Eucharist?* (Wipf and Stock, Eugene, OR, 2018) pp.126-127.

[121] Fair reading of the rubric seems to forbid any reservation of the consecrated elements, and so it was understood by most authorities right through until the 1960s. One obvious 18th century commentator is Charles Wheatly, who approved historic ways of extending distribution to the sick, but was in no doubt that the BCP orders the remains to be consumed, with communion of the sick done by a separate celebration. (See also Newman's 1839 edition of Sparrow's 17th century *Rationale*.) However, some have attempted in the past to evade that clear meaning, as, e.g. Charles Harris on 'The Communion of the Sick' in that standard text book, W. Lowther Clarke (ed), *Liturgy and Worship: A Companion to the Prayer Books of the Anglican Communion* (SPCK, 1932), pp.541-615.

other sources, namely 'ablutions'. It is useful to keep 'consumption' and 'ablutions' in separate categories (as, e.g., *The Ritual Reason Why* (1919 edition) says that '[after the blessing comes] the consumption of what remains of the Holy Sacrament, and the ablutions follow'[122]) There are two actions – consumption and ablutions – and, of the two, consumption is ordered in **1662**, whereas ablutions, as a formal procedure, has no such authority.[123] The cleansing of vessels did not figure in Canon Law in 1604, but the modern Canon F3(2) provides 'It is the duty of the minister of every church or chapel to see that the communion plate is kept washed and clean...' and this clearly supports **1662**'s expectation that the consumption would be immediately after the service, whereas the cleaning of the vessels lay outside the liturgical procedures, to be done presumably in the vestry or even in a home. Nevertheless, in the 20th century common linguistic usage assimilated both actions under the single title 'ablutions', and the outcome became the scrupulous cleansing of the vessels to ensure that neither crumb nor drop of consecrated elements remained.[124] However, the rubrics throughout revision continued to refer to the elements being 'consumed'; and 'ablutions' never entered the official currency until, in CW, the opening 'General Notes' aired the 'ministry of the deacon' which might include 'a part in...the ablutions'.[125]

There was also a change of place in the order. In the late 19th century, consumption with scrupulous ablutions began to follow immediately

---

[122] Charles Walker (rev. T.I.Ball), *The Ritual Reason Why* (Mowbray, London 1919) Qu. 395, p.140

[123] An everyday illustration is provided in any family where a parent says to a child 'finish up your dinner', and that is done at the table, whereas taking and cleaning the plate is a wholly separate action, done in the kitchen or utility room.

[124] Thus Vernon Staley wrote: 'A complete consumption of "that which was consecrated" cannot be effected without the aid of the ablutions.' (*Ceremonial of the English Church*, 4th edition, Mowbray, London, 1911, p.224) – an exact example of 'assimilation', in which ablutions invade the sphere of consumption.

[125] This is reinforced in *Common Worship: Ordination Services, Study Edition* (CHP, 2007), pp.26, 48 and 72, where the' deacon of the rite' may 'supervise the ablutions'.

upon the distribution.[126]   This was a daring following of Roman Catholic practice, and was popularly known as 'TARPing' – i.e. 'Taking Ablutions in the Roman [or Right] Place'.[127]   'Ablutions' was built into the linguistic currency by this sort of usage. However **1928** and at least some pre-War guides to ceremonial practice retained the **1662** requirement that the consumption (a term which stoutly remained) should come after the blessing. **1928** added its own variant:

If any of the consecrated Bread and Wine remain, apart from that which may be reserved for the Communion of the sick, it shall not be carried out of the Church, but the Priest and such other...[as in 1662]

It was this rubric, together with the opening rubrics of the Alternative Order for the Communion of the Sick, which rang the death-knell of the 1928 Book.[128]

The change came with S1/65, the adaptation of IntrmRt, and was repeated in S2/65. The rubric after the blessing read:

What remains of the consecrated bread and wine which is not required for purposes of Communion, shall be consumed immediately after all have communicated either by the Priest, or by one of the other ministers,

---

[126] None of the discussion here touches upon taste and sensitivity. But Kenneth Stevenson was not alone when he wrote 'We are also learning that it is unsightly (and, to the liturgically uneducated, irreverent) to watch clergy and ministers gulp down the remains in the sight of all' (in Michael Perham (ed), *Liturgy for a New Century* (SPCK/Alcuin, 1991) p.39).

[127] Roman Catholic practice was formed (a) through a general usage whereby only the priest received communion, and it was logical then briefly to cleanse the vessels immediately to round off the action, (b) through the taking of any remaining consecrated wafers to the tabernacle then (rather than have them still on the altar when the mass was over). Even when there was a distribution of the communion, the wine was traditionally not given to the communicants so that the cup needed minimal cleansing; thus anglo-catholics developed complex procedures with little precedent in Rome – but Rome provided the 'Right Place' in the rite!

[128] A slightly obscure feature of **1928**, not often noticed, was that it allowed reservation only after the Alternative Order. If **1662** were used (its text preceded **1928** in the Book), its rubric provided no exception to the consumption.

while the Priest continues the service; or it shall be left upon the holy
Table until the end of the service and then consumed.

Herein lay a policy. The phrase '*not required for purposes of Communion*'
appears at sight as a kind of tautology, simply stating that the bread and
wine remaining has been '*not required*', and is now to be consumed. But
it quickly got quoted in another sense by diocesan chancellors (led by
Garth Moore), approving the installation of aumbries or other containers
for reservation – the point being that reservation was '*for purposes of*
Communion', and so, the rulings decreed, the rubric legitimized the
retention of the consecrated elements (thus validating provision of
aumbries etc). It was not often argued, as it could have been, that in
the 1960s (and until 1983) there was no lawful provision for giving
communion from reserved elements, so the closing rubric could hardly
permit reservation '*for purposes of Communion*' of this sort.

This 1960s rubric above seems to preclude, what **1662** specified, that
lay communicants may help to consume remains, (though the rubric
perhaps allows them to assist in consuming after the service). A change
was needed, and the passive '*is...consumed*' then became the regular
terminology, so that **S3/73** and **RtA/80** in the ASB have the simpler:

Any consecrated bread and wine which is not required for purposes of
communion is consumed at the end of the administration, or after the
service.

With the coming of extended communion for the sick from 1983
onwards, the 'purposes' were now genuinely being met by reservation. The
rubric has run on unchanged (save for the substitution of '*distribution*'
for '*administration*') into CW, and it is printed now at the end of the
distribution and not after the service as previously.[129]   It is also printed

---

[129] It is more than possible that the practice of consuming at the end of the distribution has

there (though with a marginally amended text) in OrdTwo etc. More on reservation itself follows in chapter 16 below.

16. Reservation

'Reservation' is the formal term for the retention of consecrated elements at the end of a service, whereby they are not consumed as **1662** directed, but are 'reserved'. As noted in chapter 15, from 1966 onwards a closing rubric directed that bread and wine '*not required for purposes of communion*' should still be consumed, but the wording opened a door to reserving bread and wine which would yet serve the 'purposes of communion'. Until 1983 there was no legal basis for administering such bread and wine to the sick, but then communion of the sick from a celebration of communion at a distance in space and perhaps in time from the main celebration was permitted, and the term 'extended communion' came into use. 'Reservation' as a term had no official standing, and the ASB-type provision in 1983 for communicating the sick by extension, without touching on how or where the elements are retained if there is a time-gap between the original celebration and the distribution, simply directed how to distribute the elements, and the same is true in **CW** *Pastoral Services*. Similarly the provision in *Times and Seasons* for distributing on Good Friday elements consecrated the night before at the Maundy Thursday celebration, says nothing about the retention or storage of them overnight. And even the provision for 'Thanksgiving for Holy Communion' on the Thursday after Trinity, a date fixed in direct imitation of Corpus Christi in the Church of Rome, provides only for a straight celebration of the eucharist. Furthermore, the low-profile rite for *Public Worship with Communion by Extension*, provided in 2000 for

---

become the more widespread of the alternatives, perhaps assisted by the location of the rubric. It can lead to a presbyter apparently quaffing large quantities of wine from one or more upturned chalices *coram populo*, while the congregation awaits the resumption of the service. On the other hand, where the ministers receive communion last (see chapter 9 above), their own communion can well include a discreet consumption of all that remains.

'exceptional' use by the bishop's permission when there is special need, also does not use the term 'reserve'. Neither the rite nor the appended 'Bishops' Guidelines' (pp.32-33) give any indication of how the elements should be guarded, stored or carried – the sole guidance is that there should be 'a minimal interval of time between the two services' (*viz* the original celebration and the communion by extension). Whatever extra-liturgical use may anywhere be made of consecrated elements, there is no hint of official encouragement for such use in that 'minimal interval' allowed in these various permissions.[130]

The considerations above leave the storage question entirely open. Although parishes may apply for faculties for special furniture in which to keep consecrated elements within the church building, yet the rubrics and guidance are fully met by the use of a locked cupboard or safe without any visible highlighting of the chosen location.

Appendix: The Common Texts

ICET was formed in 1968, and, after sounding out different English-speaking Churches, it recommended 'Common Texts', in three editions of *Prayers We Have in Common* in 1970, 1971, and 1975.[131]   The hope was that these would be adopted by all mainstream liturgical Churches. Later, after the coming of inclusive language, ELLC provided a revised

---

[130] The title 'Thanksgiving for the Institution of Holy Communion' was invented for the 1928 BCP to avoid using 'Corpus Christi', though its new title combined with its date made its purpose clear. A curious cosmetic reassurance was accorded to the doubting by a harmless balancing provision, 'Thanksgiving for Holy Baptism' (both occasions came, without dates, in the Lesser Feasts at the back of the Book). The ASB gave a minimal mention of observing the day (p.21), with propers re thanksgivings for both baptism and holy communion on pp.918-922. The term 'Corpus Christi' reappeared in the **CW** Calendar and in the *Times and Seasons* and *Festivals* provision (and in the Church of England's annual almanacs). The festival is found in the collects and post-communions of **CW** (and even in the rules for transference on p.529). All these are, however, without any hint of extra-liturgical ceremonies connected with the eucharist, such as are practised in the Church of Rome. The non-event of Thanksgiving for the Institution of Holy Baptism, which never had a date in the calendar, and probably had no actual celebration, has quietly disappeared.
[131] The first two editions were published by Geoffrey Chapman (London, Dublin and Melbourne), the third by SPCK, London.

set of texts in *Praying Together* (Canterbury Press, 1990). The texts usually found in the eucharist were: (1) Gloria in Excelsis, (2) Kyries, (3) Nicene Creed, (4) Sursum Corda), (5) Sanctus and Benedictus qui Venit, (6) Agnus Dei, and (7) the Lord's Prayer. The varying texts of (4) are shown on p.92 above, while (2),(5) and (6) have all been adopted throughout the modern language texts, and have remained unchanged with the coming of inclusive language.[132]　　How the Church of England has varied the other texts is shown in this table.

Title	ICEL 1970	S3/73	ICEL 1975	RtA/80	ELLC 1990	CW/00
Gloria in Excelsis Line 2	and peace to his people on earth	and peace to his people on earth	and peace to his people on earth	and peace to his people on earth	and peace to God's people on earth	and peace to his people on earth
Nicene Creed Lines 14-15	by the power of the Holy Spirit he was born of the Virgin Mary and became man	by the power of the Holy Spirit he was born of the Virgin Mary and became man	by the power of the Holy Spirit he became incarnate from the Virgin Mary, and became man	by the power of the Holy Spirit he became incarnate of the Virgin Mary, and became man	was incarnate of the Holy Spirit and the Virgin Mary and became truly human	was incarnate from the Holy Spirit and the Virgin Mary and became man
Lord's Prayer Line 2	holy be your name	hallowed be your name	hallowed be your name	hallowed be your name	hallowed be your name	hallowed be your name
Lines 9-10	do not bring us to the test	do not bring us to the time of trial	save us from the time of trial	lead us into temptation	save us from the time of trial	lead us not into temptation
	but deliver us...	but deliver us...	and deliver us...	but deliver us...	and deliver us...[133]	but deliver us...

The Lord's Prayer has been minimally 'modified' in its traditional wording, to read in line 1 'who art', in line 5 'on earth', and in line 8 'those who'. This modified text is used in traditional language modern rites (save in **RtA/80** BCP-Order and **CW/00**(OrdTwo)), and in all modern-language rites since 1987 it has appeared as an alternative alongside or after the modern text.[134]

---

[132] The alternative modern Agnus Dei originates in Geoffrey Cuming's imaginative rendering in the 'modernized Series 2' in *Modern Liturgical Texts* (see pp. above).

[134] The date 1987 reflects a non-synodical decision to introduce it, and printings of **RtA/80** thereafter carried parallel columns. A detailed account of the revision until 1987 is in Colin Buchanan,

[133] Note on p.333 of the main **CW** Book allows 'on suitable occasions' the use of this ecumenical text, which is itself printed there on p.106.

Part 3:
Conclusion

We have told a complicated story of the revision of the Church of England's official liturgical texts of the eucharist within our time, but there is so much more that we could have said, about far-reaching developments marching alongside the textual revision:

- the electronic revolution, from a Commission with a wholly manual (and amateur) infra-structure to a process where texts are exchanged electronically both internationally and round a meeting table, and made available on the Church of England website in a format ready for screening in churches.
- how church members have become more aware of what they are doing in the eucharist.
- the need for formation, links between the liturgy and spiritual growth, the continuing work of Praxis.
- The effect of new rites on traditional eucharistic ceremonial,
- differing presiding personalities and styles, much enhanced by the advent of women as presbyters,
- the integration of different ministries and spiritual gifts, music, art and architecture.
- the relationships of those on the Commission with one another, or with poets, writers and musicians, with the Bishops and groups within Synod, with publishers and the secular press, looking at the relationships between finance, commercial interests.
- the importance of language, ancient and modern, translated (from Greek, Latin, Hebrew, Syriac) or newly composed, and how we translate other current languages such as British sign language, Farsi, Gujarati, Polish, etc.
- the lack of resources at different points in this story, the Cinderella treatment

---

The Lord's Prayer in the Church of England (Grove Worship Booklet 131, Grove Books, Cambridge, 1994).

of liturgy at every level, the need for more academic research and teaching in the UK.

• how worshippers have reacted to the changing character of eucharistic celebrations.

Our history is but a skeleton, and readers will recognize it as such, and perhaps enlarge upon it. We stand in a continuum of development, as Ronald Jasper said of the ASB 'I have always regarded the ASB as a pioneering work, a catalyst, a necessary step towards the creation of something even better'[1] The story does not end until we join those many with whom we have worked in face-to-face worship in a register which is not 1662, ASB or CW, but the language of heaven. Alleluia!

Select Bibliography

NB: Limits of space mean that the authorized services and the other official publications to which constant reference is made within this Study (usually with their General Synod reference numbers) are not listed here, but can fairly easily be traced if needed, and the actual listing here is necessarily highly selective. Not all titles quoted in reference in the text can be included, but their details are given where they are quoted.

Contemporary account of the revision of the eucharist (online via Grove Books):

Colin Buchanan (ed), *News of Liturgy* (monthly from January 1975 to December 2003)

Historical account chronicled:

Colin Buchanan, *Liturgical Revision in the Church of England* (Grove Booklet on Ministry and Worship 14, Grove Books, 1973) (also supplements: *14a* (1973-74), *14b* (1974-76), *14c* (1976-78), and Grove Liturgical Study 39 (1978-84)

David Hebblethwaite, *Liturgical Revision in the Church of England 1984-2004: The Working of the Liturgical Commission* (Alcuin/GROW Joint Liturgical Study 57, Grove Books, Cambridge, 2004)

The larger context of the Church of England's worship until 1980:

Geoffrey Cuming, *A History of Anglican Liturgy* (2nd ed MacMillan, London & Basingstoke, 1982)

Ronald Jasper, *The Development of Anglican Liturgy 1662-1980* (SPCK, London, 1989)

Specific studies:

Colin Buchanan, *The New Communion Service: Reasons for Dissent* (Church Book Room Press, London, 1966)

— *The End of the Offertory: An Anglican Study* (Grove Liturgical Study 14, Grove Books, Bramcote, 1978)

— *Eucharistic Consecration in Common Worship* (Grove Worship Booklet 217, Grove Books, Cambridge,2014)

— *An Evangelical Among the Anglican Liturgists* (Alcuin/SPCK, London, 2009)

— (jt with Trevor Lloyd), *Six Eucharistic Prayers as Proposed in 1996: The Official Texts for Final Approval with Introduction and Commentary* (Grove Worship Booklet 136, Grove Books, Cambridge, 1996)

Arthur Couratin (ed): *E.C.Ratcliff: Liturgical Studies* (SPCK, 1976)

Mark Dalby, *Anglican Missals and their Canons: 1549, Interim Rite and Roman* (Alcuin/ GROW Joint Liturgical Study 41, Grove Books, Cambridge, 1998)

Gregory Dix, *The Shape of the Liturgy* (Dacre, London, 1945)

David Frost, *The Language of Series 3* (Grove Booklet on Ministry and Worship 12, Grove Books, Bramcote, 1973)

Ronald Jasper (ed), *The Eucharist Today: Studies in Series 3* (SPCK, London, 1974)

Lambeth Conference 1958 (SPCK, London, 1958)

Liturgical Commission, *A Commentary on Series 3* (SPCK, London, 1971)

Bryan Spinks, *The Sacrifice of Praise; Studies…in honour of Arthur Hubert Couratin* (CLV, Editioni Liturgiche, Rome, 1981)

Companions

Paul Bradshaw (ed), *A Companion to Common Worship* (Vol.1, SPCK, London, 2001)

Colin Buchanan, Trevor Lloyd and Harold Miller (eds), *Anglican Worship Today* (Collins, London, 1980)

Mark Earey and Gilly Myers (eds), *Common Worship Today* (HarperCollins, London, 2001 – also softback in Study Edition from St John's College, Nottingham, 2006)

Charles Hefling and Cynthia Shattuck (eds) *The Oxford Guide to the Book of Common Prayer* (Oxford, New York, 2006)

Ronald Jasper and Paul Bradshaw, *A Companion to the Alternative Service Book* (SPCK, London, 1986)

Liturgical Commission, *The Alternative Service Book 1980: A Commentary by the Liturgical Commission* (CIO, London, 1980)